EASY

DOS, 3rd Edition

Shelley O'Hara

Easy DOS, 3rd Edition

Copyright © 1993 by Que® Corporation

Library of Congress Catalog No.: 93-86747

ISBN: 1-56529-640-0

95 94 93   6 5 4 3 2 1

Interpretation of the printing code: the rightmost double-digit number is the year of the book's printing; the rightmost single-digit number, the number of the book's printing. For example, a printing code of 93-1 shows that the first printing of the book occurred in 1993.

Screen reproductions in this book were created using Collage Plus from Inner Media, Inc., Hollis, NH.

Easy DOS is based on MS-DOS Version 6.2.

Publisher: David P. Ewing

Director of Publishing: Michael Miller

Managing Editor: Corinne Walls

Marketing Manager: Ray Robinson

Printer: Shepard Poorman Communications Corp.

Trademarks

All terms mentioned in this book that are known to be trademarks or service marks have been appropriately capitalized. Que cannot attest to the accuracy of this information. Use of a term in this book should not be regarded as affecting the validity of any trademark or service mark.

IBM is a registered trademark of International Business Machines Corporation.

Lotus and 1-2-3 are registered trademarks of Lotus Development Corporation.

Microsoft Excel, Microsoft Publisher, Microsoft Word, Microsoft Works, MS-DOS, and PowerPoint are registered trademarks and Microsoft Windows is a trademark of Microsoft Corporation.

WordPerfect is a registered trademark of WordPerfect Corporation.

Credits

Publishing Manager
Shelley O' Hara

Production Director
Kathie-Jo Arnoff

Acquisitions Editor
Sarah Browning

Production Editors
Lori Lyons
Cindy Morrow

Technical Editor
Michael Watson

Book Designer
Amy Peppler-Adams

Novice Reviewer
Melissa Keegan

Editorial Assistants
Jill Stanley
Michelle Williams

Production Team
Angela Bannan
Danielle Bird
Charlotte Clapp
Anne Dickerson
Karen Dodson
Bob LaRoche
Michelle Worthington
Lillian Yates

Indexers
Joy Dean Lee
Johnna VanHoose

About the Author

Shelley O'Hara is a Publishing Manager at Que Corporation. She is the author of 17 books in the Easy series, including the best-selling *Easy WordPerfect*, *Easy Windows*, and *Easy 1-2-3*. She is also the coauthor of *Real Men Use DOS*. Ms. O'Hara received her bachelor's degree from the University of South Carolina and her master's degree from the University of Maryland.

Contents at a Glance

Introduction 1

The Basics..11

Task/Review 27

Reference 197

Index 219

Contents

Introduction 1

   What Is DOS? 2

   Why You Need This Book 5

   How This Book Is Organized 5

   How To Use This Book 6

   Where To Get More Help 10

The Basics 11

   Understanding Your Computer System 12

      More on Floppy Disks 13

      More on Floppy Disk Drives 14

      More on Hard Disks 15

   Using Your Keyboard 15

   Understanding Disk Organization 18

      Directories and Files 18

      Root Directory and the Path 19

      File Names 20

      Wild Cards 20

      Special Files 22

      DOS Versions 23

      The Shell 23

   Typing a Command 24

   Taking Care of the Computer 24

Task/Review **27**

Alphabetical Listing of Tasks 28

Learning DOS Basics 31

    Start DOS 32

    Restart DOS...34

    Turn off the computer 36

    Set the prompt to display the current directory..........38

    Get help 40

    Display additional help information...........................42

    Search for a help topic..44

    Exit help 46

    Display files...48

    Clear the screen 50

    Display a wide file listing 52

    Make a directory 54

    Change directories..56

    Change to the root directory 58

    Display the directory tree 60

    Remove a directory 62

    Pause a file listing 64

    Display selected files..66

    Display directories only 68

Working with Disks 71

    Insert a disk...72

    Format a disk 74

Change drives 76

Copy a disk 78

Working with Files 83

Display file contents 84

Copy a file 86

Copy a file to another directory 88

Copy a group of files to another directory 90

Copy all files to a different drive 92

Rename a file 94

Delete a file 96

Delete all files 98

Undelete a file 100

Protecting Your Files 103

Start the Microsoft Backup program 104

Configure the Microsoft Backup program 106

Back up selected directories 112

Back up selected files 116

Restore files 120

Exit the Microsoft Backup program 122

Scan for viruses 124

Tell DOS to scan for viruses automatically 126

Customizing and Optimizing Your Computer 129

Display a volume label 130

Change a volume label 132

Check the DOS version 134

Check disk space and memory 136

Set the date 138

Set the time 140

Set the path 142

Check memory information................................. 144

Optimize memory 146

Defragment a disk 148

Using the DOS Shell.. 151

Start the DOS Shell 152

Make a menu selection 154

Exit the DOS Shell 156

Get help 158

Display files in another directory 160

Expand directories.. 162

Collapse directories 164

Expand all directories 166

Select a drive 168

Display selected files... 170

Sort files 172

Select a file 174

Select multiple files... 176

Select all files 178

Copy a file 180

Rename a file.. 182

Move a file... 184

Delete a file 186

View file contents 188

Search for a file 190

Create a directory 192

Remove a directory 194

Reference **197**

Quick Reference 198

Error Messages 198

Software Guide 200

Glossary 215

Index **219**

Introduction

- What Is DOS?

- Why You Need This Book

- How This Book Is Organized

- How To Use This Book

- Where To Get More Help

What Is DOS?

With a personal computer, you can type professional-looking letters, draw a map to your house, create letterheads, balance your checkbook, create charts, inquire about stock prices, play games, do homework, learn to type, and so on.

To do anything on a personal computer, you need:

- Hardware

- Software

- An operating system

Hardware is the actual machine—keyboard, monitor, and system unit. Hardware refers to the items that you can see and touch.

Software refers to the programs that you run on the hardware. The words *program*, *application*, and *software* are all used inter-changeably. Sometimes the terms are combined: application program, software application. They all mean the same thing.

Think of a program as a specialist hired to perform a task. You might need an accountant to plan your budget and calculate your taxes, a typist to do mailings, an artist to create a logo, a stockbroker to quote stock prices, and so on. Rather than have a specialist, you have a program. For accounting tasks, you can use a spreadsheet program. For typing letters, you can use a word processor. You can use a drawing program to create maps and logos. Each of these programs runs on the personal computer.

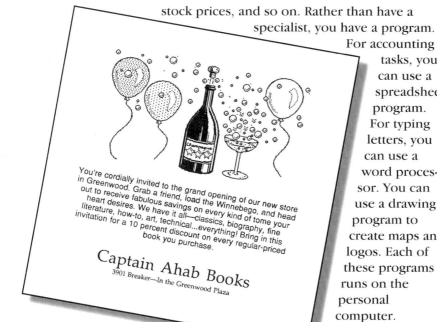

You're cordially invited to the grand opening of our new store in Greenwood. Grab a friend, load the Winnebego, and head out to receive fabulous savings on every kind of tome your heart desires. We have it all—classics, biography, fine literature, how-to, art, technical...everything! Bring in this invitation for a 10 percent discount on every regular-priced book you purchase.

Captain Ahab Books
3901 Breaker—In the Greenwood Plaza

The operating system is the link between the hardware and the software. The operating system, called *DOS* (disk operating system), manages files and runs programs.

You cannot accomplish anything without DOS. The computer and programs are useless. With DOS itself, you can do some things (copy files, for instance). When you add programs, however, you can do all kinds of things (as previously described).

MEMORANDUM

TO: All Employees
FROM: Melissa Lowery
DATE: December 29, 1991

RE: New In-House Illustrator

I am pleased to announce that Susan Trautman has recently joined our staff as an in-house illustrator.

For the past two years, Susan has been working as a free-lance illustrator, and her outstanding drawings have enhanced several of our best-selling children's books. Most recently, Susan's work has graced *Peter Goes to the Salad Bar* and *Zachary Meets the Baby Sitter*.

Susan's experience includes over a decade of illustration and layout experience in both the publishing and advertising fields. We are all excited about the possibilities opened to us by bringing Ms. Trautman on our staff full-time.

Please join me in welcoming Susan to the McBryer Publishing staff.

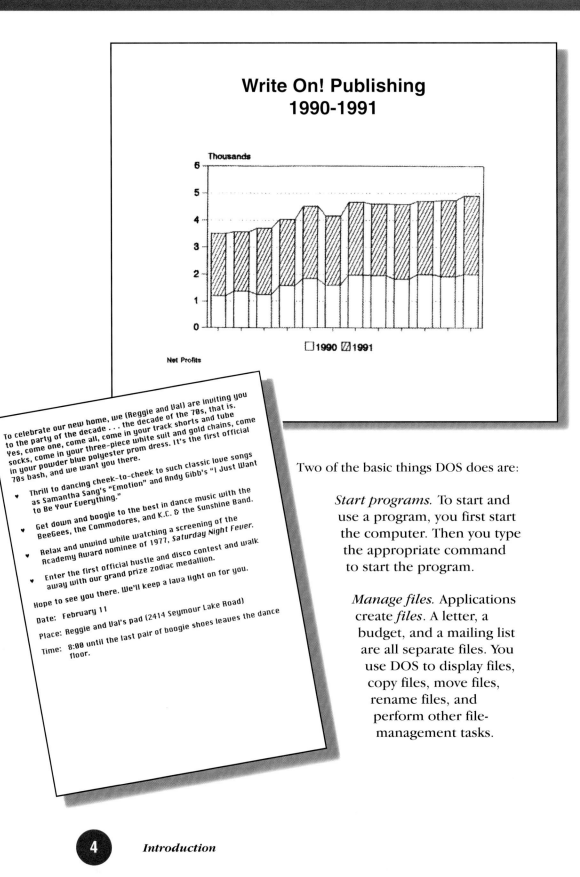

Write On! Publishing
1990-1991

Thousands

□1990 ▨1991

Net Profits

To celebrate our new home, we (Reggie and Val) are inviting you to the party of the decade . . . the decade of the 70s, that is. Yes, come one, come all, come in your track shorts and tube socks, come in your three-piece white suit and gold chains, come in your powder blue polyester prom dress. It's the first official 70s bash, and we want you there.

♥ Thrill to dancing cheek-to-cheek to such classic love songs as Samantha Sang's "Emotion" and Andy Gibb's "I Just Want to Be Your Everything."

♥ Get down and boogie to the best in dance music with the BeeGees, the Commodores, and K.C. & the Sunshine Band.

♥ Relax and unwind while watching a screening of the Academy Award nominee of 1977, *Saturday Night Fever*.

♥ Enter the first official hustle and disco contest and walk away with our grand prize zodiac medallion.

Hope to see you there. We'll keep a lava light on for you.

Date: February 11

Place: Reggie and Val's pad (2414 Seymour Lake Road)

Time: 8:00 until the last pair of boogie shoes leaves the dance floor.

Two of the basic things DOS does are:

Start programs. To start and use a program, you first start the computer. Then you type the appropriate command to start the program.

Manage files. Applications create *files*. A letter, a budget, and a mailing list are all separate files. You use DOS to display files, copy files, move files, rename files, and perform other file-management tasks.

Why You Need This Book

DOS is not easy to learn. You must memorize commands, and you must type the commands in an exact format (called the *syntax* of the command). DOS doesn't give you any clues about how to proceed. You only see a small prompt (C:\>, for instance). To use programs, you MUST learn some basic DOS commands.

But don't worry. This book is designed to make learning DOS *easy*. This book helps the beginning DOS user perform basic operations. You don't need to worry that your knowledge of computers is limited. This book teaches you all you need to know for basic operations.

You don't need to worry that you might do something wrong and ruin a program or the computer. This book points out mistakes you might make and shows you how to avoid them. This book explains what to do when you change your mind—how to escape from a situation.

Reading this book will build your confidence. It will show you what steps are necessary to get a particular job done.

Remember: DOS does only what you tell it to do. Don't tell it to delete a file unless you would do the same thing manually (that is, send the only remaining copy of that file through a shredder).

How This Book Is Organized

This book is designed with you, the beginner, in mind. The book is divided into several parts:

- Introduction

- The Basics

- Task/Review

- Reference

This "Introduction" explains how the book is set up and how to use the book.

The next part, "The Basics," outlines general information about your computer and its keyboard layout. This part explains basic terms and concepts.

The main part of this book, "Task/Review," tells you how to perform a particular task. The first task explains how to start DOS.

The "Reference Guide" includes a quick reference list of the most common DOS commands, a guide to error messages, a software guide that defines the different application programs you can use on the computer, and a glossary of common computer terms.

How To Use This Book

This book is set up so that you can use it several different ways:

- You can read the book from start to finish, or you can start reading at any point in the book.

- You can experiment with one exercise, many exercises, or all exercises.

- You can look up specific tasks that you want to accomplish, such as displaying a file listing.

- You can flip through the book, looking at the Before and After screens, to find specific tasks.

- You can look at the alphabetical listing of tasks at the beginning of the Task/Review part to find the task you want.

- You can read just the task, just the review, or both the task and review parts. As you learn the program, you might want to follow along with the tasks. After you learn the program, you can use the review part to remind yourself how to perform a certain task.

- You can read any part of the exercises you want. You can read all the text to see both the steps to follow and the explanation of the steps. You can read just the text in red to see only the actions to perform. You can read just the explanation to understand what happens during a particular step.

As you read, don't worry about making a mistake. For many tasks, the book explains how to undo the task. The book also points out errors that you might make and how to avoid them.

How To Follow an Exercise

For consistency, this book makes certain assumptions about how your computer is set up and how you use DOS. As you follow each exercise, keep the following key points in mind:

- This book assumes that you have a hard drive.

- This book is based on Microsoft MS-DOS Version 6.2, but you can use this book with any MS-DOS version. If a particular command is included only in DOS 6.2, this fact is noted.

- This book mainly covers using DOS from the command prompt. The first part of the Task/Review part covers the command prompt. If you have DOS 5 or 6, you also can use the DOS Shell. The second half of the Task/Review part covers using the DOS Shell to perform some common tasks. This book contains a complete section that covers using the DOS Shell to perform some of the most common tasks.

- This book shows the screens in color. Even if you have a color monitor, however, your screen display will probably appear in black and white.

Each task includes
Before and After screens
that show how the
computer screen will
look before and after
you follow the
numbered steps in the
Task section.

Task section

The Task section includes
numbered steps that tell you
how to accomplish certain
tasks, such as copying a file.
The numbered steps walk
you through a specific
example so that you can learn
the task by doing it. Blue text
below the numbered steps
explains the concept in more
detail.

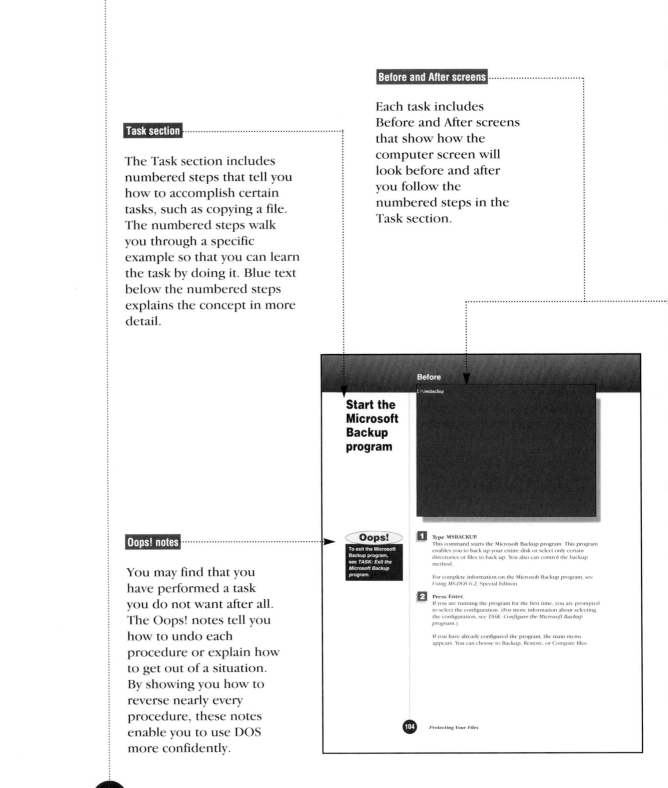

Before

C:\>msbackup

**Start the
Microsoft
Backup
program**

Oops!

To exit the Microsoft
Backup program,
see *TASK: Exit the
Microsoft Backup
program.*

1 **Type MSBACKUP.**
This command starts the Microsoft Backup program. This program
enables you to back up your entire disk or select only certain
directories or files to back up. You also can control the backup
method.

For complete information on the Microsoft Backup program, see
Using MS-DOS 6.2, Special Edition.

2 **Press Enter.**
If you are running the program for the first time, you are prompted
to select the configuration. (For more information about selecting
the configuration, see *TASK: Configure the Microsoft Backup
program.*)

If you have already configured the program, the main menu
appears. You can choose to Backup, Restore, or Compare files.

104 *Protecting Your Files*

Oops! notes

You may find that you
have performed a task
you do not want after all.
The Oops! notes tell you
how to undo each
procedure or explain how
to get out of a situation.
By showing you how to
reverse nearly every
procedure, these notes
enable you to use DOS
more confidently.

After you learn a procedure
by following a specific
example, you can refer to the
Review section for a quick
summary of the task. The
Review section gives you the
generic steps for completing
a task so that you can apply
the steps to your own work.
You can use these steps as a
quick reference to refresh
your memory about how to
perform procedures.

After

Alert

Backup requires configuration
for this computer.

▶ Start Configuration   Quit

Note

DOS 6 and 6.2 include
a Microsoft Windows
version of the Backup
program. See *Using
MS-DOS 6.2*, Special
Edition for help on this
program.

Other notes

The extra margin
notes explain a little
more about each
procedure. These
notes define terms,
explain other
options, and refer
you to other
sections, when
applicable.

REVIEW

1 Type **MSBACKUP**.

2 Press **Enter**.

Note

The MSBACKUP com-
mand is only available
with DOS 6 and 6.2.

Note

A *backup* is an extra
set of the data and
programs on your hard
disk. If something
happens to the original
copy, you can use the
backup to restore the
data and programs.

Start the Microsoft Backup Program **105**

Where To Get More Help

This book does not cover all DOS commands. This book is geared toward the beginning user—someone who wants just the basics. This person isn't ready for advanced features, such as using the MODE command.

As you become more comfortable, you may need a more complete reference book. Que offers several DOS books to suit your needs:

MS-DOS 6.2 Quick Reference

MS-DOS 6.2 QuickStart

Using MS-DOS 6.2, Special Edition

Que also offers several books on specific software programs. Some of the most popular include the following titles:

Using 1-2-3 Release 3.4, Special Edition

Using 1-2-3 Release 4 for Windows, Special Edition

Using Quattro Pro 5.0, Special Edition

Using Quattro Pro 5.0 for Windows, Special Edition

Using WordPerfect Version 6 for DOS, Special Edition

Using WordPerfect 6 for Windows, Special Edition

The following books also will be of interest:

Introduction to Personal Computers, 4th Edition

Que's Computer User's Dictionary, 4th Edition

The Basics

- Understanding Your Computer System

- Using Your Keyboard

- Understanding Disk Organization

- Typing a Command

- Taking Care of the Computer

Understanding Your Computer System

Your computer system is made up of these basic parts:

- The system unit

- The monitor

- The keyboard

- The floppy disk drive(s)

- The hard disk drive

You may also have a mouse and a printer.

System Unit   The system unit is the box that holds all the electrical components of your computer. The floppy disk drive and hard disk drive are also usually inside the system unit. (The size of the system unit varies.) Usually the power switch is on the back or side of the box.

Monitor   The monitor displays on-screen what you type on the keyboard. Your monitor also may have a power switch.

Keyboard   You use the keyboard to communicate with the computer. You use it to type entries and issue commands. You type on the keyboard just as you do on a regular typewriter. A keyboard also has special keys that you use. (Different computers have different keyboards.) These keys are discussed later in the section *Using Your Keyboard*.

Floppy Disk Drive   The floppy disk drive is the door into your computer. It allows you to put information on the computer—onto the hard drive—and to take information off the computer—onto a floppy disk.

Hard Disk Drive   A hard disk drive stores the programs and files with which you work.

Mouse   The mouse is a pointing device that enables you to move the mouse pointer on-screen, select windows, and issue commands.

Printer   The printer makes a paper copy (called a "hard copy") of the documents that you create on the computer. To print, you need to attach and install a printer.

More on Floppy Disks

There are two sizes of floppy disks:

- 5 1/4-inch disks

- 3 1/2-inch disks

Your drive uses one size or the other. If you have a 5 1/4-inch drive, use 5 1/4-inch disks. If you have a 3 1/2-inch drive, use 3 1/2-inch disks. Your computer may have two drives—a 5 1/4- and a 3 1/2-inch drive.

Floppy disks differ in size as well as in the amount of information they can store. The amount of information, which is called *capacity*, is measured in kilobytes (abbreviated K) or in megabytes (abbreviated M). One byte equals about one typed character. One kilobyte equals around 1 thousand bytes (1024 to be exact), and one megabyte equals around 1 million bytes.

5 1/4-inch disks come in two capacities: 360K and 1.2M. 360K disks often are called double-sided double-density (DD). This disk can store around 360,000 characters of information. 1.2M disks often are called double-sided high-density (HD). This type of disk can store 1.2 million bytes. (Double-sided means that both sides of the disk store information—like a phonograph record.)

3 1/2-inch disks come in three capacities: 720K, 1.44M, and 2.88M. 720K disks often are called double-density or double-sided double-density (DD). This disk can store around 720,000 characters of information. 1.44M disks often are called double-sided high-density (HD). This type of disk can store 1.44 million bytes. The newest floppy size is 2.88M. This disk can store 2.88 million bytes.

The disk drive you have must match the disk type you use. If you have a drive that can "read" only 360K disks, you can use only 360K disks. If you have a drive that can "read" 1.44M disks, then you should use only 1.44M disks. The high-density disk drives (1.2M 5 1/4-inch and 1.44M 3 1/2-inch) can read and write both disk capacities. In general, however, you should use the disk type for your drive.

Disks generally are blank when you purchase them. (A few companies sell preformatted disks.) To prepare a disk for use, you must format it. (See *TASK: Format a disk* in the Task/Review part.) Keep in mind that you must format a disk to the correct capacity. That is, you shouldn't take a 360K disk and format it as a 1.2M disk.

More on Floppy Disk Drives

Your computer has at least one floppy disk drive. You may have more than one. The first floppy disk drive is named drive A, the second, drive B. The hard disk is named drive C.

Drive A

Drive C

Drive B

More on Hard Disks

A hard disk is similar to a floppy disk in that it stores information, but a hard disk is much larger and much faster than a floppy disk. A small hard disk might be as much as 25 times larger than a floppy disk. Hard disks are measured in megabytes (M or meg) and come in various sizes: 20M, 30M, 40M, 60M, 80M, 100M, and up.

A hard disk is also hard (rather than floppy) and is usually encased in the system unit. (You also can add an external hard drive.) Some programs require a hard disk, and this book assumes that you have one.

Using Your Keyboard

To communicate with DOS, you type commands at the keyboard. A computer keyboard is just like a typewriter, only a keyboard has additional keys:

- Arrow and other movement keys (Home, PgUp, PgDn, End)

- Function keys (F1-F10 or F1-F12)

- Text editing keys (Backspace, Del, Ins)

- Modifier keys (Shift, Ctrl, Alt)

- Enter

- Other special keys (Print Screen, Scroll Lock, and so on)

Original PC keyboard

AT keyboard

Enhanced keyboard

The Basics

For the following keyboard examples, this book uses the Enhanced keyboard. Your keyboard has the same keys, although they might be in a different location. You can familiarize yourself with the keyboard by reading the names on the keys.

These keys are located in different places on different keyboards. For example, sometimes the function keys are across the top of the keyboard. Sometimes they are on the left side of the keyboard.

Different keys perform different actions, depending on the program you are using. In general, the keys perform the following basic functions:

Arrow and other movement keys. In a program, these keys enable you to move around on-screen or select text. Other keys, such as Home, PgUp, PgDn, and End, also move the cursor in programs. (Nothing happens when you press these keys at the DOS prompt.)

Function keys. Function keys initiate commands in programs. The command initiated depends on the program. In WordPerfect, for example, pressing F6 makes text bold.

Editing keys (Backspace, Ins, Del). Backspace deletes characters to the left of the cursor. Del works the same way, only it deletes characters at the cursor location and then to the right of the cursor.

Modifier keys (Shift, Ctrl, and Alt). You can use these keys to modify the action of a function key. For example, pressing F6 in Word-Perfect tells the program you want to make text bold. Pressing and holding down Shift and then pressing F6 (Shift-F6) tells WordPerfect that you want to center text. The commands assigned to each key and key combination vary from program to program.

Shift also has an additional, more traditional use—it makes lowercase text uppercase (much like on a typewriter).

Enter. This key confirms a command. You also can use it to insert a carriage return when you are typing text.

Understanding Disk Organization

When you first turn on the computer (called "booting" the computer), DOS is loaded or started. (If you want to follow along, turn on the computer. See *TASK: Start DOS* in the Task/Review part.) You see a blank screen with a small prompt—usually C:/. This prompt is intimidating—it offers no clue on what to do next. What's behind that blank screen?

Directories and Files

Think about how you store items in your office. In your office, you may have a filing cabinet. In that filing cabinet, you probably have folders that pertain to different projects, clients, patients, or some other grouping—maybe logical, maybe not. Within each folder you have articles, letters, diagrams, reports—anything that you want to save. This storage method carries over to DOS.

With DOS, a disk is like a filing cabinet. Within that disk, you have directories—areas set aside for certain files (such as memos, articles, or diagrams). The same items that you store in a folder are stored in electronic form in a file. That file is then stored in a directory.

Root Directory and the Path

The main directory is called the *root directory*. All other directories are branches of this directory, much like the roots of a tree. Directories can contain files, programs, or other directories. The root directory is designated by a backslash (\).

To get to a particular file, you must trace the path from the root directory to the directory that contains the file. The path is the list of directories, starting with the root. Each directory name is separated by a backslash (\). For example, the path

```
C:\WORD\REPORTS
```

gives you these directions: start at drive C, go from the root directory (\) to WORD, and then go to REPORTS.

The structure looks like this:

File Names

Each file must have a unique or different name. An entire file name is made up of the file name (up to eight characters) and the extension (optional three characters). The file name and extension are separated by a period. You cannot use these characters in a file name:

> " / \ [ ] : ;

REPORT.DOC is a valid file name. REPORT is the file name, and DOC is the extension. The file name should tell you what the report contains; the extension often tells you the type of file. Some programs assign an extension automatically.

MY NOTES is not a valid file name because a file name cannot contain spaces. If you want to include a space in a file name, however, you can use the underline character instead (MY_NOTES).

EASYDOSBOOK.DOC also is not a valid file name because it contains too many characters.

Wild Cards

When you want to work with a group of files, you can use wild cards. There are two types of wild cards: an asterisk and a question mark.

An asterisk wild card (*) matches any characters. The most common use of this wild card is *.*. You might hear other computer users describe this wild card as star-dot-star. This file spec matches all files; that is, the file can have any root name and any extension. (A *file spec* is a combination of the path, file name, and extension.)

The file spec *.TXT specifies files with any root name (*.) and the extension TXT. The following files would be included in this group:

> CHAP1.TXT
>
> MEMO.TXT
>
> RESUME.TXT

The following files wouldn't be included (because they have a different extension):

> CHAP1.DOC
>
> SALES.XLS

The question mark wild card (?) matches any single character. For instance, the file spec ?SALES.DOC includes all files that start with any character; the remaining letters must be SALES, and the file must have the extension DOC. The following files would be included in this group:

ESALES.DOC

WSALES.DOC

SSALES.DOC

NSALES.DOC

The following files wouldn't be included:

SWSALES.DOC (? matches only one character)

ESALES.XLS (extensions don't match)

You can use wild cards in different combinations to control which files are included in a group.

Suppose, for example, that you are writing a book that has eight chapters. The file for each chapter is named CHAP, followed by the chapter number, a period, and the file extension DOC. When you want to copy all the files (CHAP1.DOC through CHAP8.DOC), you can use a file spec such as

CHAP?.DOC

This file spec uses the ? wild card and tells DOS to include every file named CHAP that is followed by one character and has a DOC extension. Remember that each ? wild card represents one character.

If, however, your book is 15 chapters long, and the files are named CHAP1.DOC through CHAP15.DOC, you need to use a different wild card—the asterisk. To copy all the files for this book, you can use a file spec such as

CHAP*.DOC

This file spec tells DOS to include every file named CHAP, followed by any number of characters, with a DOC extension. Remember that the * wild card represents any number of characters.

Special Files

Your computer contains some special files that you should understand.

To process commands, you must have a file called COMMAND.COM. This is a special DOS file. When you install DOS on a disk, this file is copied to the hard drive.

When you first start DOS, it looks for a file called AUTOEXEC.BAT. This file must be stored in the root directory. When DOS starts and finds the file, it executes the file. This file may include commands that control different settings. For example, you might include a command that tells DOS where your programs are located. This command is called a *path command*.

The following shows a simple AUTOEXEC.BAT file:

```
PROMPT $P$G
PATH C:\DOS;C:\WP51
```

This file changes your prompt (C:\) so that it displays the current subdirectory. For example, if you are in the directory DATA, which is a subdirectory of C:\WP51, you would see

```
C:\WP51\DATA>
```

The PATH command tells DOS to look in the DOS and WP51 directories for program files.

Another special file that DOS uses to start is CONFIG.SYS, a configuration file. Some applications require special commands. These commands are contained in the CONFIG.SYS file.

The following shows a simple CONFIG.SYS file:

```
FILES=20
BUFFERS=25
```

These settings control how DOS uses files. Some programs require that these are set to a certain value.

When dealing with these files, keep these rules in mind:

- Don't delete any of these files: COMMAND.COM, AUTOEXEC.BAT, or CONFIG.SYS.

- Don't try to change the contents of COMMAND.COM.

- As you add applications to the computer, the program manual might tell you to make changes to the AUTOEXEC.BAT file or the CONFIG.SYS file. You must use a special text editor to modify these files. Be careful when making any changes. You should understand each command in the file before changing anything.

DOS Versions

You may have heard DOS called MS-DOS or PC DOS. For all practical purposes, they are the same. DOS is DOS.

DOS is updated periodically: new commands are added, other commands are made to work better, and bugs (problems) are fixed. The most current DOS is Version 6.2. This book is based on Microsoft MS-DOS 6.2.

The Shell

DOS 5 and 6 include a shell. (DOS 4 also had a shell, but it worked differently.) The *shell* is a program that acts as a user interface to DOS. Rather than use the command line to enter commands, you can enter commands through the shell. A shell is not included with DOS 6.2. If the DOS 5 or 6 shell exists in your DOS directory, the DOS 6.2 upgrade version will allow you to continue using it. The shell is available separately on the MS-DOS 6.2 Supplemental Disk.

```
┌──────────────────────── MS-DOS Shell ─────────────────────────┐
│ File   Options   View   Tree   Help                           │
│ C:\                                                            │
│ ⌹A   ⌹B   ■C              ↘                                   │
├───────── Directory Tree ──────────┬─────── C:\*.*  ───────────┤
│ ┌┐ C:\                         ↑  │ ▭ AUTOEXEC .BAT      247  06-28-91 ↑│
│  ├─┬ 123R23                       │ ▭ COMMAND  .COM   47,867  03-08-91 │
│  ├─┬ AFTERDRK                     │ ▭ CONFIG   .SYS      256  06-25-91 │
│  ├─┬ AMIPRO                       │ ▭ DEFAULT  .BAK    1,797  08-07-91 │
│  ├─┐ COLLAGE                      │ ▭ FONTWID  .BAT       50  07-26-90 │
│  ├─┐ DOS                          │ ▭ HIMEM    .SYS   11,304  05-01-90 │
│  ├─┬ EXCEL                        │ ▭ IMAGE    .BAK   94,208  09-05-91 │
│  ├─┐ EZDFIGS                      │ ▭ IMAGE    .DAT   94,208  09-05-91 │
│  ├─┬ EZFIGS                       │ ▭ NDOS     .COM   11,845  06-06-91 │
│  ├─┐ FONTS                        │ ▭ NDOS     .OVL   73,612  06-06-91 │
│  ├─┬ HG3                          │ ▭ TREEINFO.NCD     1,883  09-05-91 │
│  ├─┐ MOUSE1                       │ ▭ VP       .BAT      128  01-29-91 │
│  ├─┐ NORTON                       │ ▭ WINA20   .386    9,349  03-08-91 │
│  ├─┐ PCFILE                    ↓  │                                  ↓│
├───────────────────────── Main ───────────────────────────────┤
│ ▭ Command Prompt                                             ↑│
│ ▭ Editor                                                      │
│ ▭ MS-DOS QBasic                                               │
│ ▦ Disk Utilities                                              │
│                                                               │
│                                                              ↓│
├───────────────────────────────────────────────────────────────┤
│ F10=Actions   Shift+F9=Command Prompt              9:55a      │
└───────────────────────────────────────────────────────────────┘
```

The shell is less intimidating and easier to use than the command prompt. The shell is covered in the last section of the Task/Review part.

Typing a Command

Learning DOS is similar to learning a new language. You have to communicate by using words that DOS understands. DOS then takes these words or commands and translates them into a language that the physical components of the machine can understand.

The language you use is called *syntax*. Syntax is the proper format of a command. If you don't get the syntax correct, the command will not work. As you work through the exercises in this book, be careful to type the command (and any spaces) as they appear. If the command doesn't work as discussed, try typing the command again.

Case doesn't matter when you type a command. You can type the command in upper- or lowercase letters. DOS reads COPY, copy, and Copy as the same command.

If you make a mistake when typing, you can press Backspace to delete characters before you press Enter.

Taking Care of the Computer

Take care of the hardware (everything you can see and touch) the same way you would care for your TV or VCR. Don't feed it, water it, drop it, or expose it to extreme heat or cold.

Take care of the software the same way you would take care of audio or video cassettes. Don't leave them in extreme heat, don't spill anything on them, don't open the metal shutter, and keep them away from magnets. Keep in mind that all electrical equipment puts out a magnetic field. This means the telephone, the electric pencil sharpener, and even the personal computer itself. Of course, you don't have to keep your phone in a desk drawer—just don't keep floppy disks near the phone.

Finally, always turn off your machine properly. Never shut off your computer while in the middle of a program:

Close any open programs and be sure that you are at the DOS prompt. Then you can turn off your computer:

```
C:\>
```

Task/Review

- Learning DOS Basics

- Working with Disks

- Working with Files

- Protecting Your Files

- Customizing and Optimizing Your Computer

- Using the DOS Shell

Alphabetical Listing of Tasks

Command Tasks

Back up selected directories 112

Back up selected files 116

Change a volume label 132

Change directories 56

Change drives 76

Change to the root directory 58

Check disk space and memory 136

Check memory information 144

Check the DOS version 134

Clear the screen 50

Configure the Microsoft Backup program 106

Copy a disk 78

Copy a file 86

Copy a file to another directory 88

Copy a group of files to another directory 90

Copy all files to a different drive 92

Defragment a disk 148

Delete a file 96

Delete all files 98

Display a volume label 130

Display a wide file listing 52

Display additional help information 42

Display directories only 68

Display file contents 84

Display files 48

Display selected files 66

Display the directory tree 60

Exit help 46

Exit the Microsoft Backup program..122

Expand all directories 166

Expand directories...162

Format a disk 74

Get help 40

Insert a disk..72

Make a directory...54

Optimize memory 146

Pause a file listing..64

Remove a directory 62

Rename a file...94

Restart DOS..34

Restore files..120

Scan for viruses 124

Search for a help topic..44

Set the date 138

Set the path...142

Set the time 140

Set the prompt to display the current directory...................................38

Sort files 172

Start DOS 32

Start the Microsoft Backup program...104

Tell DOS to scan for viruses automatically 126

Turn off the computer 36

Undelete a file 100

DOS Shell Tasks

Collapse directories 164

Copy a file 180

Create a directory 192

Delete a file 186

Display files in another directory 160

Display selected files 170

Exit the DOS Shell 156

Expand all directories 166

Expand directories 162

Get help 158

Make a menu selection 154

Move a file 184

Remove a directory 194

Rename a file 182

Search for a file 190

Select a drive 168

Select a file 174

Select all files 178

Select multiple files 176

Sort files 172

Start the DOS Shell 152

View file contents 188

Learning DOS Basics

This section includes the following tasks:

- Start DOS
- Restart DOS
- Turn off the computer
- Set the prompt to display the current directory
- Get help
- Display additional help information
- Search for a help topic
- Exit help
- Display files
- Clear the screen
- Display a wide file listing
- Make a directory
- Change directories
- Change to the root directory
- Display the directory tree
- Remove a directory
- Pause a file listing
- Display selected files
- Display directories only

Start DOS

Oops!

If you don't see the DOS prompt, be sure that you turned on both the computer and monitor. If you have plugged the computer and monitor into a power strip, be sure that the strip is plugged in and is turned on.

1 **Turn on the computer and monitor.**
Every computer has a different location for its On/Off switch. Check the side, the front, and the back of your computer. Your monitor may have a separate On/Off switch; if so, you must turn this switch to On.

DOS starts automatically when you turn on your computer. You might see information on-screen as DOS goes through its start-up routine. Some systems check the memory. You might see something like 256 OK, 512 OK, and so on. You might see different commands on-screen.

DOS starts and then looks for a CONFIG.SYS file. If DOS finds this file, it executes the commands in that file. Then DOS looks for an AUTOEXEC.BAT file. If it finds this file, it executes the commands in that file. (These files are discussed in the Basics part.)

On some systems, you simply have to turn on the computer. Other systems, however, prompt you for the date and time. In this case, follow steps 2 and 3.

2 **If you are prompted for the date, type the current date and press Enter.**
When you first turn on the computer, some systems ask you to enter the current date.

After

```
C:\>
```

3 **If you are prompted for the time, type the current time and press Enter.**

If you are prompted for the date, you will also be prompted for the time.

You see the DOS prompt on-screen (C:\>). The DOS prompt may appear differently on your computer. (You can change the prompt if you want. See *TASK: Set the prompt to display the current directory*.)

REVIEW

1 Turn on the computer and monitor.

2 If you are prompted, type the current date and press **Enter**.

3 If you are prompted, type the current time and press **Enter**.

> **Note**
>
> If you see the error message Non-System disk or disk error. Replace and press any key when ready, you probably have a floppy disk in drive A. Eject this disk and press any key. If this doesn't work, you may have a problem with your disk. See *Using MS-DOS 6.2,* Special Edition, for more information.

> **Note**
>
> Your computer uses the date and time to keep track of when you save files to disk. Therefore, if the date and time information isn't entered automatically, be sure to enter the correct date and time so that your file information is accurate.

Restart DOS

Oops!

If nothing happens
when you press these
keys, turn off the
machine and then
turn it on again.

1 **Press and hold down Ctrl, Alt, and Del.**
You must press all three keys at once. That is, press and
hold down the Ctrl key. Keeping Ctrl held down, press and
hold down the Alt key. Then keeping Ctrl and Alt held
down, press the Del key. Pressing these three keys together
tells DOS to start over.

(The Before screen shows a spreadsheet application that "froze"
and wouldn't respond to commands.)

2 **Release all three keys.**
This process is called a "warm boot" or a "soft boot."
DOS runs through its start-up routine and executes the
AUTOEXEC.BAT file and CONFIG.SYS. In a warm boot, DOS
skips some of the checks it performs during a "cold boot."
(A cold boot is when you turn off and then turn on the
machine.) A cold boot is harder on your computer. Always
try a warm boot first.

Some computers also have a Reset button. You can press this
button to restart the computer.

After

```
C:\>
```

REVIEW

Press **Ctrl-Alt-Del**.

Note

If the system "hangs" (doesn't respond to your commands), you may need to restart. Also, if you change a key file (CONFIG.SYS or AUTOEXEC.BAT), you must reboot to make the changes take effect.

Note

Be careful! Using Ctrl-Alt-Del is an escape from some situations, but you should reboot only when nothing else works or only when a program tells you to do so.

Turn off the computer

```
C:\>
```

Oops!

To turn on the computer, see *TASK: Start DOS*.

1 **Exit all programs.**
You should turn off the computer only when you are at a DOS prompt. If you are working in a program, save all files and exit the program before you turn off the computer. (See your program manual for help with saving and exiting.)

2 **Turn off the computer and the monitor (if necessary).**
Every computer has a different location for its On/Off switch. Check the side, the front, and the back of your computer. Your monitor may have a separate On/Off switch. If so, you also need to turn this switch to Off.

After

REVIEW

 Exit all programs so that you return to the DOS prompt.

2 Turn off the computer and monitor.

Note

Should you leave your computer on? One-half of the computer world says you should leave the computer on most of the time. The other half says you should turn it off each time you finish using it. Each practice has its own benefits. See *Using MS-DOS 6.2,* Special Edition, for more information.

```
C>PROMPT $P$G
```

Set the prompt to display the current directory

Oops!

Type PROMPT, and then press Enter to see just the C> prompt.

 Type PROMPT.
PROMPT is the command that tells DOS what to display when it is ready for a command. The default prompt is C>. If you or someone else has changed your PROMPT command, your prompt might look different.

 Press the space bar once.
Pressing the space bar once inserts a space between the command and the prompt you want to use.

3 **Type PG.**
PG is a code that tells DOS to display the current directory. When you change directories, the name of the current directory appears.

Suppose that you change to the DATA directory. The prompt will read C:\DATA>. This prompt reminds you where you are within DOS.

 Press Enter.
Pressing Enter confirms the new prompt. You still see C:\> at the root level, but when you move to a different directory, you see that directory name.

After

```
C>PROMPT $P$G

C:\>
```

REVIEW

1 Type **PROMPT**.

2 Press the **space bar once**.

3 Type **PG**.

4 Press **Enter**.

Note

You can type anything for the prompt (step 3)—for instance, you can type a greeting (Hi Mike!), a reminder, or any text you want.

Note

You should add a prompt statement to your AUTOEXEC.BAT file so that you don't have to set the prompt each time you start DOS. See *Using MS-DOS 6.2,* Special Edition, for more information.

Get help

```
C:\>HELP
```

Oops!

To exit help, see
TASK: Exit Help.

1 **Type HELP.**
This is the command to access the Help topics.

2 **Press Enter.**
This step executes the command. You see a list of DOS commands on-screen. The menu options (File and Search) along the top of the screen enable you to access Help commands.

3 **Press the ↓ key until you highlight Copy.**
This step selects the command for which you want help.

4 **Press Enter.**
This step displays a description of the command and the proper syntax of the command. Syntax is the format in which you must type the command. If you use incorrect syntax, the command will not execute.

As a shortcut, you can also type **HELP** and then type the name of the command you want. If you type **HELP COPY** and press Enter, for example, DOS displays help on the copy command

After

```
 File  Search                                              Help
                        MS-DOS Help: COPY
◄Notes► ◄Examples►

                              COPY

Copies one or more files to another location.

This command can also be used to combine files. When more than one file is
copied, MS-DOS displays each filename as the file is copied.

Syntax

    COPY [/A¦/B] source [/A¦/B] [+ source [/A¦/B] [+ ...]][destination
    [/A¦/B]] [/V]

Parameters

source
    Specifies the location and name of a file or set of files from which you
    want to copy. Source can consist of a drive letter and colon, a
    directory name, a filename, or a combination.

<Alt+C=Contents> <Alt+N=Next> <Alt+B=Back>              C  00001:002
```

REVIEW

1 Type **HELP**.

2 Press **Enter**.

3 Use the arrow keys to highlight the topic you want.

4 Press **Enter**.

Note

To display other information (Notes and Examples), see *TASK: Move among help information.*

Note

This help system is available only with Versions 6 and 6.2 of DOS.

Display additional help information

```
 File  Search                                              Help
                      ┌─ MS-DOS Help: COPY ─┐
│◄Notes► ◄Examples►                                             ▲│
│─────────────────────────────────────────────────────────────│
│                           COPY                               │
│Copies one or more files to another location.                │
│                                                              │
│This command can also be used to combine files. When more than one file is│
│copied, MS-DOS displays each filename as the file is copied.  │
│                                                              │
│Syntax                                                        │
│                                                              │
│    COPY [/A¦/B] source [/A¦/B] [+ source [/A¦/B] [+ ...]][destination│
│    [/A¦/B]] [/V]                                             │
│                                                              │
│Parameters                                                    │
│                                                              │
│source                                                        │
│    Specifies the location and name of a file or set of files from which you│
│    want to copy. Source can consist of a drive letter and colon, a│
│    directory name, a filename, or a combination.            ▼│
│<Alt+C=Contents> <Alt+N=Next> <Alt+B=Back>       │ C  00001:002│
```

Oops!

To return to the previous topic, press the Alt-B key combination. To display the next topic, press Alt-N. To return to the contents screen, press Alt-C.

 Display help on the Copy command.
For information on this step, see *TASK: Get help*. By default, DOS displays the Syntax of the command. You also can display Notes and Examples.

Syntax displays the format of the command. Notes explain any additional information about the command. Examples shows you some example commands.

The first option, Notes, is selected. To select a different option, press Tab.

2 **Press Enter.**
This step selects the Notes option. You see a screen with additional information.

After

```
┌──────────────── MS-DOS Help: COPY--Notes ─────────────────┐
│ ◀Examples▶  ◀Syntax▶                                      ↑│
│ ─────────────────────────────────────────────────────────│
│                                                           │
│                      COPY—Notes                           │
│                                                           │
│ Copying to and from devices                               │
│                                                           │
│ You can substitute a device name for one or more occurrences of source or │
│ for destination.                                          │
│                                                           │
│ Using or omitting the /B switch when copying to a device  │
│                                                           │
│ When destination is a device (for example, COM1 or LPT1), the /B switch │
│ causes MS-DOS to copy data to the device in binary mode. In binary mode, all │
│ characters (including such special characters as CTRL+C, CTRL+S, CTRL+Z, and │
│ carriage return) are copied to the device as data. Whereas, omission of the │
│ /B switch causes MS-DOS to copy data to the device in ASCII mode. In ASCII │
│ mode, such special characters as those previously listed may cause MS-DOS to │
│ take special action during the copying process.           │
│                                                           │
│ Using the default destination file                       ↓│
├───────────────────────────────────────────┬───────────────┤
│ ⟨Alt+C=Contents⟩ ⟨Alt+N=Next⟩ ⟨Alt+B=Back⟩ │ C  00001:002  │
└───────────────────────────────────────────┴───────────────┘
```

REVIEW

1 Display help on the command you want.

2 Press **Tab** to select another option (Notes, Examples, or Syntax).

3 Press **Enter**.

Note

See *TASK: Exit Help* for information on exiting help.

Note

This help system is available only with Versions 6 and 6.2 of DOS.

Search for a help topic

```
 File  Search                                                    Help
┌──────────────── MS-DOS Help: Command Reference ────────────────┐
│Use the scroll bars to see more commands. Or, press the PAGE DOWN key. For
│more information about using MS-DOS Help, choose How to Use MS-DOS Help
│from the Help menu, or press F1.
│
│⟨ANSI.SYS⟩            ⟨Fc⟩                 ⟨Net Time⟩
│⟨Append⟩              ⟨Fcbs⟩              ⟨Net Use⟩
│⟨Attrib⟩              ⟨Fdisk⟩             ⟨Net Ver⟩
│⟨Break⟩               ⟨Files⟩             ⟨Net View⟩
│⟨Buffers⟩             ⟨Find⟩              ⟨Nlsfunc⟩
│⟨Call⟩                ⟨For⟩               ⟨Path⟩
│⟨Chcp⟩                ⟨Format⟩            ⟨Pause⟩
│⟨Chdir (cd)⟩          ⟨Goto⟩              ⟨Power⟩
│⟨Chkdsk⟩              ⟨Graphics⟩          ⟨POWER.EXE⟩
│⟨Choice⟩              ⟨Help⟩              ⟨Print⟩
│⟨Cls⟩                 ⟨HIMEM.SYS⟩         ⟨Prompt⟩
│⟨Command⟩             ⟨If⟩                ⟨Qbasic⟩
│⟨Copy⟩                ⟨Include⟩           ⟨RAMDRIVE.SYS⟩
│⟨Country⟩             ⟨Install⟩           ⟨Rem⟩
│⟨Ctty⟩                ⟨Interlnk⟩          ⟨Rename (ren)⟩
│⟨Date⟩                ⟨INTERLNK.EXE⟩      ⟨Replace⟩
│⟨Dblspace⟩            ⟨Intersvr⟩          ⟨Restore⟩
⟨Alt+C=Contents⟩ ⟨Alt+N=Next⟩ ⟨Alt+B=Back⟩           C  00006:002
```

Oops!

If DOS cannot find a match, you see the message, Match not found. Press Enter, check your typing, and try again.

1 **Type HELP and press Enter.**

This step displays the Help Contents screen.

2 **Press Alt-S.**

This step opens the Search menu. To press the Alt-S key combination, press and hold down the Alt key. Then type S. Release both keys.

3 **Type F.**

This step selects the Find command. You see the Find dialog box, and DOS prompts you, Find What? Note that you can control how the search is performed.

To use the other available search options, see *Using MS-DOS 6, Special Edition.*

4 **Type MEM.**

MEM is the command on which you want help. You also can type the text you want to find. Suppose, for example, that you don't know the name of a specific command but you do know you want information on memory; you can simply type memory.

DOS searches first through the main topics and then scans the other help text to find a match.

After

```
 File  Search                                          Help
┌─────────────────────────────────────────────────────────┐
│            ── MS-DOS Help: MEM ──                         │↑
│ ◄Notes► ◄Examples►                                       │
│ ─────────────────────────────────────────────────────── │
│                          MEM                              │
│ Displays the amount of used and free memory in your system.│
│                                                           │
│ You can use the MEM command to display information about allocated memory │
│ areas, free memory areas, and programs that are currently loaded into │
│ memory.                                                   │
│                                                           │
│ Syntax                                                    │
│                                                           │
│    MEM [/CLASSIFY¦/DEBUG¦/FREE¦/MODULE modulename] [/PAGE] │
│                                                           │
│ To display the status of your system's used and free memory, use the │
│ following syntax:                                         │
│                                                           │
│    MEM                                                    │
│                                                           │
│ Switches                                                  │↓
│─────────────────────────────────────────────┬───────────│
│<Alt+C=Contents> <Alt+N=Next> <Alt+B=Back>   │ C  00001:002│
└─────────────────────────────────────────────┴───────────┘
```

5 **Press Enter.**
This step starts the search. DOS displays information about the
command on-screen.

REVIEW

1 Type **HELP** and press **Enter** to start Help.

2 Press **Alt-S** to open the Search menu.

3 Type **F** to select the Find command.

4 Type the command or text you want to find.

5 Press **Enter**.

Note

To cancel the search,
press the Esc key.

Note

To exit Help, see
TASK: Exit Help.

Exit help

```
  File  Search                                              Help
┌─────────────────────── MS-DOS Help: MEM ────────────────────────┐
│ ◄Notes►  ◄Examples►                                             ↑│
│ ─────────────────────────────────────────────────────────────── │
│                                                                  │
│                              MEM                                 │
│                                                                  │
│ Displays the amount of used and free memory in your system.      │
│                                                                  │
│ You can use the MEM command to display information about allocated memory │
│ areas, free memory areas, and programs that are currently loaded into │
│ memory.                                                          │
│                                                                  │
│ Syntax                                                           │
│                                                                  │
│    MEM [/CLASSIFY|/DEBUG|/FREE|/MODULE modulename] [/PAGE]        │
│                                                                  │
│ To display the status of your system's used and free memory, use the │
│ following syntax:                                                │
│                                                                  │
│    MEM                                                           │
│                                                                  │
│ Switches                                                         ↓│
├──────────────────────────────────────────────┬──────────────────┤
│ ⟨Alt+C=Contents⟩ ⟨Alt+N=Next⟩ ⟨Alt+B=Back⟩   │  C   00001:002   │
└──────────────────────────────────────────────┴──────────────────┘
```

Oops!

To restart help, type
HELP and press
Enter.

1 **From any Help screen, press Alt-F.**
This step opens the File menu. You see a list of File commands.

2 **Type x.**
This step selects the Exit command. You exit Help and return to the DOS prompt.

After

```
C:\>HELP
C:\>
```

Note

For information on all Help options, see *Using MS-DOS 6.2*, Special Edition.

Note

This help system is available only with Versions 6 and 6.2 of DOS.

REVIEW

 1 Press **Alt-F** to open the Help menu.

2 Type **x** to select the Exit command.

Display files

```
C:\>DIR
```

 From the DOS prompt, type DIR.
DIR is the directory command. It tells DOS to list all the files in the current directory. In this example, the current directory is the root (or main directory). See *TASK: Change directories* for information on changing the directory.

2 **Press Enter.**
Pressing Enter confirms the command. You see a list of the files and directories in the root directory. (Your list will vary, depending on the files and directories you have created.)

Notice that the following information appears on-screen:

File name	The root of the file name (up to eight characters) appears first.
Extension	The extension is listed in the second column.
File Size	The next column lists the size of the file. The size is measured in bytes. One byte equals about one character. If the entry is a directory, nothing is listed.
Directory	If the entry is a directory, you see <DIR> in the next column.

After

```
C:\>DIR

 Volume in drive C is SEO'S DISK
 Directory of  C:\

HARDCARD      <DIR>      9-04-91  12:10a
DOS           <DIR>      5-18-91  12:16a
CONFIG   SYS       10  10-23-90   1:02a
AUTOEXEC OLD       98   9-04-91  12:49a
DATA          <DIR>      9-04-91  12:39a
COMMAND  COM    25307   3-17-87  12:00p
AUTOEXEC BAT      128   8-28-91  12:02a
TREEINFO NCD      299   9-04-91  12:18a
FRECOVER DAT    38912  10-12-91  12:00a
FRECOVER BAK    38912  10-12-91  12:00a
COLLAGE       <DIR>      8-28-91  12:01a
WORD5         <DIR>      5-18-91  12:03a
NU            <DIR>      5-18-91  12:17a
CHOICE        <DIR>      5-18-91  12:20a
WP51          <DIR>      5-18-91  12:23a
QPRO          <DIR>      6-24-91   2:46a
       16 File(s)    4431872 bytes free

C:\>
```

Date   The next column displays the date when the file was created or modified.

Time   The final column displays the time when the file was created or modified.

The two lines at the end of the directory listing display the number of files, bytes taken, and bytes free (disk space remaining).

The DOS prompt appears at the bottom of the listing so that you can type the next command.

REVIEW

 From the DOS prompt, type **DIR**.

 Press **Enter**.

Note

If files scroll off the screen (you cannot see the entire list), you have too many files to display on one screen. In this case, display a wide listing (see *TASK: Display a wide file listing*) or pause the display (see *TASK: Pause a file listing*).

Clear the screen

```
C:\>DIR

 Volume in drive C is SEO'S DISK
 Directory of  C:\

HARDCARD     <DIR>       9-04-91  12:10a
DOS          <DIR>       5-18-91  12:16a
CONFIG   SYS       10  10-23-90   1:02a
AUTOEXEC OLD       98   9-04-91  12:49a
DATA         <DIR>       9-04-91  12:39a
COMMAND  COM    25307   3-17-87  12:00p
AUTOEXEC BAT      128   8-28-91  12:02a
TREEINFO NCD      299   9-04-91  12:18a
FRECOVER DAT    38912  10-12-91  12:00a
FRECOVER BAK    38912  10-12-91  12:00a
COLLAGE      <DIR>       8-28-91  12:01a
WORD5        <DIR>       5-18-91  12:03a
NU           <DIR>       5-18-91  12:17a
CHOICE       <DIR>       5-18-91  12:20a
WP51         <DIR>       5-18-91  12:23a
QPRO         <DIR>       6-24-91   2:46a
          16 File(s)   4431872 bytes free

C:\>CLS
```

Oops!

If you see the message Bad command or file name, you typed the command incorrectly. Try again.

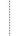 **From the DOS prompt, type CLS.**
This step tells DOS to clear the screen.

2 **Press Enter.**
Pressing Enter confirms the command. The current screen information is cleared so that all you see is the DOS prompt at the top of the screen.

After

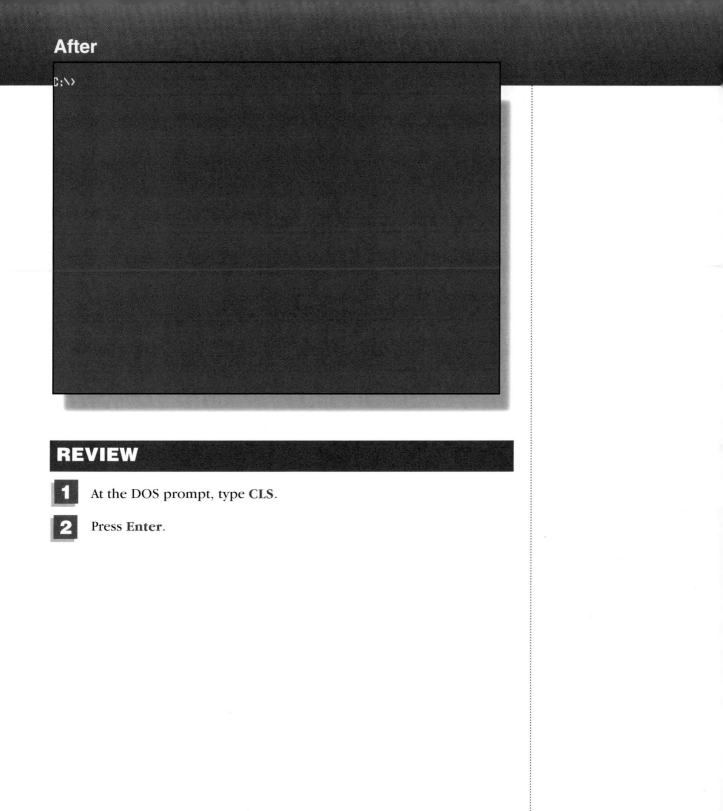

```
C:\>
```

1 At the DOS prompt, type **CLS**.

2 Press **Enter**.

`C:\>DIR /W`

Display a wide file listing

1 **From the DOS prompt, type DIR.**
DIR is the directory command. Typing this command tells DOS to display a directory listing.

2 **Press the space bar once.**
Pressing the space bar once inserts a space between the command name and the switch. A switch is added to a command to modify how the command works.

3 **Type /W.**
/W is a switch. Switches are preceded by a slash and modify the command (DIR). In this case, the switch tells DOS to display a wide listing (W). The entire command is DIR /W.

4 **Press Enter.**
Pressing Enter confirms the command. You see a listing across the screen of the directory contents. (Depending on what files and directories you have created, you will see something different.)

Note that only the file or directory name is listed in five columns across the screen. The other file information (size, date, and time) does not appear. In DOS 6 and 6.2, directories appear in brackets. Also in DOS 6 and 6.2, the last two lines display the number of files, number of bytes used, and number of bytes free.

After

```
C:\>DIR /W

 Volume in drive C is HARD DISK
 Volume Serial Number is 1724-0637
 Directory of C:\

[HARDCARD]      [DOS]           CONFIG.SYS      [OLD_DOS.1]     WINA20.386
AUTOEXEC.BAT    TREEINFO.NCD    FRECOVER.DAT    FRECOVER.BAK    [COLLAGE]
[WORD5]         [NU]            [CHOICE]        [WP51]          COMMAND.COM
[QPRO]
        16 file(s)      135489 bytes
                       2744320 bytes free

C:\>
```

REVIEW

 At the DOS prompt, type **DIR /W**.

 Press **Enter**.

Make a directory

```
C:\>MD \DATA
```

1 **At the DOS prompt, type MD.**
MD is the make directory command. Typing this command tells DOS to create a directory.

2 **Press the space bar once.**
Pressing the space bar once inserts a space between the command name and the directory name.

3 **Type \DATA.**
DATA is the name of the directory that you want to create. The backslash tells DOS to make this a directory of the root directory. (The backslash represents the root.)

4 **Press Enter.**
Pressing Enter confirms the command; DOS creates the directory. The entire command is MD\DATA. Keep in mind that the directory you started from is still the current directory. You return to the DOS prompt.

5 **Type DIR and press Enter.**
This step displays the directory listing on-screen so that you can see the new directory entry.

After

```
Volume in drive C is HARD DISK
Volume Serial Number is 1724-0637
Directory of C:\

HARDCARD     <DIR>        09-04-91   12:10a
DOS          <DIR>        05-18-91   12:16a
CONFIG   SYS          74  09-04-91   12:49a
DATA         <DIR>        09-04-91   12:24a
OLD_DOS  1   <DIR>        09-04-91   12:39a
WINA20   386        9349  04-09-91    5:00a
AUTOEXEC BAT          98  09-04-91   12:49a
TREEINFO NCD         299  09-04-91   12:18a
FRECOVER DAT       38912  09-04-91   12:00a
FRECOVER BAK       38912  09-04-91   12:00a
COLLAGE      <DIR>        08-28-91   12:01a
WORD5        <DIR>        05-18-91   12:03a
NU           <DIR>        05-18-91   12:17a
CHOICE       <DIR>        05-18-91   12:20a
WP51         <DIR>        05-18-91   12:23a
COMMAND  COM       47845  04-09-91    5:00a
QPRO         <DIR>        06-24-91    2:46a
       17 file(s)       135489 bytes
                       2711552 bytes free

C:\>
```

Note

New directories are created within the current directory if you don't type the entire path. For instance, if you forget the backslash, the directory is placed in the current directory—which may not be the root directory.

Note

To change directories, see *TASK: Change directories.*

REVIEW

 1 At the DOS prompt, type **MD**.

2 Press the **space bar once**.

3 Type the complete name of the directory (including the backslash and the path).

 4 Press **Enter**.

Change directories

```
C:\>CD\DATA
```

1 **At the DOS prompt, type CD.**
CD is the change directory command. Typing this command tells DOS to change to a different directory.

2 **Press the space bar once.**
Pressing the space bar once inserts a space between the command name and the directory name.

3 **Type \DATA.**
\DATA is the directory name. If you don't have a directory with this name, type the name of a directory that you do have. (To create the DATA directory, see *TASK: Make a directory*.)

4 **Press Enter.**
Pressing Enter confirms the command. The entire command is CD\DATA.

If your prompt displays the current directory, you see C:\DATA>. This prompt reminds you that you are in the DATA directory. (Your prompt may display only C:\>. To make your prompt display the current directory name, see *TASK: Set the prompt* to display the current directory.)

After

```
C:\>CD\DATA

C:\DATA>
```

After you are in the new directory, you can display a directory listing, start a program, or copy files. CD is an important command. This command enables you to navigate around the directory structure by moving from directory to directory.

REVIEW

1 At the DOS prompt, type **CD**.

2 Press the **space bar once**.

3 Type the directory name. Be sure to type the entire path.

4 Press **Enter**.

Note

The path tells DOS where to find the directory, so you must type the entire path or route to the command. If the directory is part of another directory, you must type the entire name. For example, if DATA is contained in the directory WORD, you must type **CD \WORD\DATA**.

Note

To back up one directory (move to the directory that contains the current directory), type **CD..** (two periods). This command tells DOS to move back one directory. For instance, if you are at the C:\WP\DATA> prompt, typing **CD..** takes you to the C:\WP> prompt (directory).

Change to the root directory

`C:\DATA>CD\`

Oops!

If you see the message Bad command or file name, you might not have typed the command correctly. Try typing the command again.

1 **At the DOS prompt, type CD.**
CD is the change directory command. Typing this command tells DOS to make a different directory active.

2 **Type \.**
The backslash (\) is the name for the root directory. Typing this command tells DOS that you want to return to the root directory.

3 **Press Enter.**
Pressing Enter confirms the command. You return to the root directory.

After

```
C:\DATA>CD\

C:\>
```

Note

You can return to the root directory from any other directory by typing this command.

REVIEW

 From the DOS prompt, type **CD**.

 Press **Enter**.

Note

If you see the message `Invalid Switch`, you typed a forward slash (/) instead of a backward slash (\).

Display the directory tree

```
C:\>TREE
```

1 **Type CD\.**
This step starts you at the root directory on drive C. See *TASK: Change to the root directory* if you need help with this step.

2 **Type TREE.**
TREE is the tree directory command. Typing this command tells DOS to display only the directory names in a tree format. A tree format shows which directories contain other directories.

3 **Press Enter.**
Pressing Enter confirms the command. You see a map of your directory structure. Each directory name is listed. Directories within directories are also displayed; lines show how the directories are organized.

After

```
C:\>TREE
Directory PATH listing for Volume HARD DISK
Volume Serial Number is 1724-0637
C:.
├───HARDCARD
├──DOS
├──DATA
├──OLD_DOS.1
├──COLLAGE
│   └───FIGURES
├──WORD5
│   └───WORK
├──NU
├──CHOICE
├──WP51
│       ├───MACROS
│       ├───GRAPHICS
│       ├───MISC
│       ├───BOOK
│       └───CLASS
└──QPRO
        └───HOUSE

C:\>
```

REVIEW

 Type **TREE**.

 Press **Enter**.

Note

If you are in a directory other that the root, typing **TREE** lists the subdirectories in that directory (if any exist).

Remove a directory

`C:\>RD\DATA`

Type RD.
RD is the remove directory command. Typing this command tells DOS to remove an empty directory.

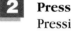
Press the space bar once.
Pressing the space bar once inserts a space between the command name and the directory name.

3 Type \DATA.
DATA is the name of the directory that you want to remove. The entire command is RD \DATA. If you do not have a directory named DATA, type the name of a directory that you do have. Make sure that it is a directory you no longer need. (To create the DATA directory, see *TASK: Make a directory*.)

Press Enter.
Pressing Enter confirms the command. The directory is removed.

Type DIR and press Enter.
This step displays a directory listing so that you can verify that the directory is removed.

After

```
Volume in drive C is HARD DISK
Volume Serial Number is 1724-0637
Directory of C:\

HARDCARD     <DIR>     09-04-91  12:10a
DOS          <DIR>     05-18-91  12:16a
CONFIG   SYS       74  09-04-91  12:49a
OLD_DOS  1   <DIR>     09-04-91  12:39a
WINA20   386     9349  04-09-91   5:00a
AUTOEXEC BAT       98  09-04-91  12:49a
TREEINFO NCD      299  09-04-91  12:18a
FRECOVER DAT    38912  09-04-91  12:00a
FRECOVER BAK    38912  09-04-91  12:00a
COLLAGE      <DIR>     08-28-91  12:01a
WORD5        <DIR>     05-18-91  12:03a
NU           <DIR>     05-18-91  12:17a
CHOICE       <DIR>     05-18-91  12:20a
WP51         <DIR>     05-18-91  12:23a
COMMAND  COM    47845  04-09-91   5:00a
QPRO         <DIR>     06-24-91   2:46a
     16 file(s)      135489 bytes
                    2621440 bytes free

C:\>
```

REVIEW

1 Type **RD**.

2 Press the **space bar once**.

3 Type the directory name.

4 Press **Enter**.

> **Note**
>
> Before you remove a directory, you must delete all files in that directory. The directory in this example (DATA) didn't contain any files. If it did, you would see an error message. In this case, delete all files. (See *TASK: Delete all files.*) Then try this task again.

> **Note**
>
> If you have trouble removing a directory, that directory might contain other directories. When you type **DEL** *.*, you delete all the files, but you don't remove the directories. You must use the RD (remove directory) command to remove the directories.

Pause a file listing

```
C:\DOS>DIR /P
```

 Type CD \DOS.
This command tells DOS to change to the directory named DOS. You should have a directory that contains your DOS file. This directory might be named something different (such as BIN). If so, type that name rather than DOS.

 Press Enter.
Pressing Enter changes the current directory to DOS. This directory contains several files. You see the prompt C:\DOS>.

 Type DIR /P.
DIR is the directory command and /P is a switch. Switches are preceded by a slash and modify the command (DIR). In this case, the switch tells DOS to display one screen of information and then pause.

 Press Enter.
Pressing Enter confirms the command. You see a list of DOS files. The message at the bottom of the file list tells you how to continue:
Press any key to continue...

 Press Enter.
Pressing Enter tells DOS to display the next screenful of information. You can press another key instead of Enter—for instance, the space bar.

After

```
Volume in drive C is HARD DISK
Volume Serial Number is 1724-0637
Directory of C:\DOS

.            <DIR>     05-18-91  12:16a
..           <DIR>     05-18-91  12:16a
EGA     SYS      4885  04-09-91   5:00a
FORMAT  COM     32911  04-09-91   5:00a
NLSFUNC EXE      7052  04-09-91   5:00a
COUNTRY SYS     17069  04-09-91   5:00a
DISPLAY SYS     15792  04-09-91   5:00a
EGA     CPI     58873  04-09-91   5:00a
BASIC   COM      1063  03-17-87  12:00p
BASICA  COM     36403  03-17-87  12:00p
HIMEM   SYS     11552  04-09-91   5:00a
KEYB    COM     14000  04 00 01   5:00a
KEYBOARD SYS    34697  04-09-91   5:00a
MODE    COM     23537  04-09-91   5:00a
SETVER  EXE     12007  09-04-91  12:49a
ANSI    SYS      9029  04-09-91   5:00a
DEBUG   EXE     20634  04-09-91   5:00a
DOSKEY  COM      5883  04-09-91   5:00a
EDLIN   EXE     12642  04-09-91   5:00a
Press any key to continue . . .
```

6 **Continue pressing Enter until all files have been displayed.**
When all files are listed, you return to the DOS prompt.

REVIEW

1 Change to the directory that you want to list.

2 Type **DIR /P**.

3 Press **Enter**.

4 Continue pressing **Enter** until all files are displayed.

Display selected files

```
C:\DOS>DIR *.SYS
```

Oops!

If you see the message File not found, no files matched the file spec you typed. Try the command again or specify other files to find.

1 Type **CD \DOS**.
This command changes to the DOS directory. The DOS directory contains DOS files. If you don't have a directory named DOS, type the name of a directory that you do have.

2 Press **Enter**.
Pressing Enter confirms the command. The current directory is now DOS.

3 Type **DIR *.SYS**.
The DIR command tells DOS to list files. The rest of the command tells DOS which files to list. In this case, the command tells DOS to list files with any file name. (The asterisk is a wild card. It matches any characters and any number of characters.) The files must have the extension SYS. *.SYS is sometimes called a file spec—it specifies which files to include.

4 Press **Enter**.
Pressing Enter confirms the command. You see only the SYS files in the directory. If the list is longer than a screenful, it will scroll off the screen.

After

```
C:\DOS>DIR *.SYS

 Volume in drive C is HARD DISK
 Volume Serial Number is 1724-0637
 Directory of C:\DOS

EGA      SYS      4885 04-09-91    5:00a
COUNTRY  SYS     17069 04-09-91    5:00a
DISPLAY  SYS     15792 04-09-91    5:00a
HIMEM    SYS     11552 04-09-91    5:00a
KEYBOARD SYS     34697 04-09-91    5:00a
ANSI     SYS      9029 04-09-91    5:00a
RAMDRIVE SYS      5873 04-09-91    5:00a
SMARTDRV SYS      8335 04-09-91    5:00a
VDISK    SYS      3455 03-17-87   12:00p
DRIVER   SYS      5409 04-09-91    5:00a
PRINTER  SYS     18804 04-09-91    5:00a
        11 file(s)      134900 bytes
                       2539520 bytes free

C:\DOS>
```

REVIEW

1 From the DOS prompt, type **DIR** followed by the file or files that you want to display. Use wild cards (* and ?) if you want.

2 Press **Enter**.

Note

If you see the message **Too many parameters,** you typed the command in the wrong format. Do not insert spaces between wild cards or the extension.

Note

Use this same procedure to list other files. For example, type **DIR S*.*** to list all files that start with S and have any extension. Type **DIR FO*.COM** to match all files that start with FO and have the extension COM. Type **DIR ASSIGN.COM** to display the file named ASSIGN.COM.

Display directories only

```
C:\>DIR *.
```

1 **From the DOS prompt, type DIR *. (period).**
This command tells DOS to display a directory (DIR). The rest of the command is the file spec; it tells DOS which files to list. The first part of the command tells DOS to display files with any name. (The asterisk is a wild card and matches any other characters.) The second part of the command tells DOS to list files with no extension (nothing following the period). Be sure to type the period.

2 **Press Enter.**
Pressing Enter confirms the command. You see a list of all files with any file name and no extension. In most cases, directories don't have extensions, so this command should display the directories on disk. (If this directory contains some files without extensions, these files also will be listed.)

After

```
C:\>DIR *.

 Volume in drive C is HARD DISK
 Volume Serial Number is 1724-0637
 Directory of C:\

HARDCARD     <DIR>     09-04-91  12:10a
DOS          <DIR>     05-18-91  12:16a
COLLAGE      <DIR>     08-28-91  12:01a
WORD5        <DIR>     05-18-91  12:03a
NU           <DIR>     05-18-91  12:17a
CHOICE       <DIR>     05-18-91  12:20a
WP51         <DIR>     05-18-91  12:23a
QPRO         <DIR>     06-24-91   2:46a
        8 file(s)            0 bytes
                       2506752 bytes free

C:\>
```

REVIEW

 From the DOS prompt, type **DIR** *. (period).

2 Press **Enter**.

Note

With DOS 5, 6, and 6.2, you also can use the command **DIR/A:D** to display all directories.

Note

If you type just **DIR*** without the period, all files and directories are listed—just as if you typed **DIR**.

Working with Disks

This section covers the following tasks:

- Insert a disk

- Format a disk

- Change drives

- Copy a disk

Insert a disk

```
C:\>A:
```

Oops!

You must shut the drive door. If the door isn't shut, the drive cannot read the disk.

 Hold the disk so that the label is facing up.
Just as you shouldn't insert a videocassette tape upside down, you also shouldn't insert a floppy disk upside down.

If you are using a 5 1/4-inch disk that doesn't have a label, hold the disk so that the notched side is on the left. (Disk types are described in the Basics part.)

If you are using a 3 1/2-inch disk that does not have a label, look for writing (disk type, arrow, manufacturer, for instance) to indicate the "up" side. Hold the disk so that you see the writing.

 Insert the disk into the drive.
Push the disk gently—don't force it. With a 3 1/2-inch disk, you should hear a click, indicating the disk is inserted (skip step 3). For 5 1/4-inch disks, you must follow an additional step (step 3).

 If necessary, shut the drive door.
The drive door has a lever or latch. Push the lever so that it is closed.

Type A: and press Enter.
This step makes floppy drive A (where you inserted the disk) active. If you inserted the disk into a different floppy disk drive (such as B), type that name instead. DOS displays A:\> to tell you that a disk is inserted properly into the drive.

After

```
C:\>A:

A:\>
```

REVIEW

  Hold the disk label up.

  Insert the disk into the drive.

3 If necessary, shut the drive door.

Note

You cannot shut the drive lever if a disk is not inserted properly into the drive (5 1/4-inch disks).

Format a disk

```
C:\>FORMAT A:
```

Oops!

To cancel the format, press Ctrl-Break for step 6 in the TASK section.

1 Insert a blank disk into drive A.
Be sure that the disk is blank (or contains information that you no longer need). Formatting wipes out all the information on the disk. For help inserting the disk, see *TASK: Insert a disk.*

2 Type FORMAT.
FORMAT is the command that prepares a disk for use.

3 Press the space bar once.
This step inserts a space between the command and the drive to format.

4 Type A:.
Drive A contains the disk that you want to format. Be sure not to format drive C.

5 Press Enter.
Pressing Enter confirms the command. You see the message Insert new diskette for drive A: and press ENTER when ready.

6 Press Enter.
Pressing Enter tells DOS that the disk has been inserted. The formatting procedure begins. Depending on your DOS version, different things may happen. When the format is complete, you see the message Format complete.

After

```
C:\>FORMAT A:
Insert new diskette for drive A:
and press ENTER when ready...

Checking existing disk format.
Saving UNFORMAT information.
Verifying 720K
Format complete.

Volume label (11 characters, ENTER for none)? DATA DISK

    730112 bytes total disk space
    730112 bytes available on disk

      1024 bytes in each allocation unit.
       713 allocation units available on disk.

Volume Serial Number is 2A34-07E7

Format another (Y/N)?
```

 7 **If prompted for a volume label, type DATA DISK for the volume label and press Enter.**
Depending on the version of DOS you are using, you may not be prompted for a volume label. This label simply assigns a name to the disk. You can press Enter to skip adding a name.

After the volume label is displayed, you see other information (total disk space, allocation units, and so on). Then you see the message Format another (Y/N)?

8 **Type N and press Enter.**
This step tells DOS that you are finished formatting. You return to the DOS prompt.

REVIEW

1 Insert a blank disk into drive A and type **FORMAT**.

2 Press the **space bar once**.

3 Type the drive name that contains the disk to format.

4 Press **Enter twice**.

5 If prompted, type a volume label and press **Enter**.

6 Type **N** and press **Enter**.

> **Note**
>
> You will not be warned if the disk that you are formatting contains information. Be sure to insert a blank disk or a disk that contains information you no longer need.

> **Note**
>
> With DOS 5, 6, and 6.2, you may be able to unformat a disk. See *Using MS-DOS 6.2*, Special Edition, for complete information.

Change drives

```
C:\>A:
```

Oops!

If you see the message Not Ready reading drive A Abort, Retry, Fail?, you may not have inserted the disk, may have in-serted it improperly, or may have forgotten to shut the drive door. Insert a disk and type R to retry.

1 **Insert a formatted disk into drive A.**
You may have just one drive. In this case, it is drive A. If you have more than one drive, drive A is usually the top drive of the computer. See *TASK: Insert a disk*.

A formatted disk is a disk that has been prepared for use. If you need to format a disk, see *TASK: Format a disk*.

2 **Type A:.**
Typing A: specifies the drive that you want to change to (drive A). The name of a drive consists of two parts: the letter and a colon. Be sure not to insert a space between the two items.

3 **Press Enter.**
Pressing Enter confirms the command. You see A:\> on-screen. This prompt reminds you that drive A is the current drive.

After

```
C:\>A:
A:\>
```

 Insert a disk into the drive.

2 Type the drive letter followed by a colon (such as **A:**, **B:**, or **C:**).

3 Press **Enter**.

Note

You need to change drives when you want to access files on another drive. For example, you might want to copy the files on the disk in drive A to drive C (or vice versa).

Note

If the disk hasn't been formatted, you see the message General failure reading A Abort, Retry, Fail? Remove the unformatted disk, and type R.

Copy a disk

```
C:\>
```

(Part 1 of 2)
Copying a disk is a two-part process. The first part, Enter the command, is covered on these two pages. Turn the page for the second part, Swap disks.

Oops!

You cannot copy a disk from one floppy drive to another floppy drive unless the disks are the same size (3 1/2- or 5 1/4-inch) and capacity.

1 **Insert a disk into drive A.**
Insert a disk that contains files you want to copy. For help inserting the disk, see *TASK: Insert a disk*.

2 **Type DISKCOPY.**
The DISKCOPY command tells DOS to copy everything on the disk. This process copies the files, the file storage information, and the tracks—technical information about how the data is stored.

3 **Press the space bar once.**
Pressing the space bar once inserts a space between the command and the drive.

4 **Type A:.**
Drive A contains the disk that you want to copy.

5 **Press the space bar once.**
Pressing the space bar inserts a space between the source disk (the disk you are copying) and the target disk (the disk you are copying to).

6 **Type A:.**
Drive A will also contain the disk to which you want to copy. You will swap disks back and forth.

After

```
C:\>DISKCOPY A: A:
```

REVIEW

 1 Insert the disk you want to copy into drive A.

 2 Type **DISKCOPY A:**.

 3 Press the **space bar once**.

 4 Type **A:**.

Copy a disk

(Part 2 of 2)
Copying a disk is a two-part process. The first part, Enter the command, is covered on the preceding two pages. These pages cover the second part, Swap Disks.

```
C:\>DISKCOPY A: A:
```

Oops!

To cancel the copy procedure, press Ctrl-Break at step 2 of the TASK section.

 Press Enter.
Pressing Enter confirms the command. You see the message `Insert SOURCE diskette in drive A: Press any key to continue.`

 Press Enter.
Pressing Enter confirms that you have inserted the source disk. (You inserted the source disk in step 1.)

You see information about the copy in progress. (For definitions of tracks and sectors, see *Using MS-DOS 6.2,* Special Edition.) DOS copies part of the disk and then prompts you to insert the target disk with the message `Insert TARGET diskette in drive A: Press any key to continue.`

3 **Eject the disk, insert the target disk, and press Enter.**
You eject a 3 1/2-inch disk by pressing the button near the disk slot. You eject a 5 1/2-inch disk by opening the drive door.

The target disk is the disk on which you want the copy placed.

4 **Continue ejecting and inserting the appropriate disk as prompted.**
Depending on how many bytes the disk holds and the amount of memory on your computer, you may have to swap disks several times. DOS 6.2 generally requires only one disk swap. When the

After

```
Insert SOURCE diskette in drive A:

Press any key to continue . . .

Copying 80 tracks
9 sectors per track, 2 side(s)

Insert TARGET diskette in drive A:

Press any key to continue . . .

Insert SOURCE diskette in drive A:

Press any key to continue . . .

Insert TARGET diskette in drive A:

Press any key to continue . . .

Volume Serial Number is 07E9-1C5B

Copy another diskette (Y/N)? N

C:\>
```

disk has been completely copied, you may see a volume serial
number. You also see the message Copy another diskette (Y/N)?

5 **Type N.**
Typing N tells DOS that you do not want to copy another disk.

REVIEW

1 Press **Enter** to confirm the command.

2 Press **Enter** to start the copy.

3 Eject the source disk and insert the target disk when prompted.

4 Continue swapping disks until the disk is copied.

5 Type **N** when prompted Copy another diskette (Y/N)? if you do not
want to copy another disk. Type **Y** if you want to copy another disk.

Note

When you purchase
new software, use this
command to make
copies of the disks;
then use only the
copies. This method
protects your original
disks.

Working with Files

This section contains the following tasks:

- Display file contents

- Copy a file

- Copy a file to another directory

- Copy a group of files to another directory

- Copy all files to a different drive

- Rename a file

- Delete a file

- Delete all files

- Undelete a file

Display file contents

Oops!

If the file scrolls off the screen, stop the file display by pressing the Ctrl-S key combination. Restart by pressing Ctrl-S again.

 1 **Type CD\ and press Enter.**
This step changes to the root directory. For help with this step, see *TASK: Change to the root directory*.

 2 **Type TYPE.**
The TYPE command tells DOS to display the contents of a file.

 3 **Press the space bar once.**
Pressing the space bar once inserts a space between the command and the file that you want to display.

 4 **Type AUTOEXEC.BAT.**
AUTOEXEC.BAT is the name of the file you want to display.

 5 **Press Enter.**
Pressing Enter confirms the command. You see on-screen the contents of the file named AUTOEXEC.BAT. (You may have different commands in your AUTOEXEC.BAT file.)

The TYPE command only displays the contents of a file. You cannot edit the file.

After

```
C:\>CD\

C:\>TYPE AUTOEXEC.BAT
ECHO OFF
PROMPT $P$G
date
time
PATH C:\DOS;C:\;C:\NU;c:\WORD5;C:\WP51;c:\collage
FR /SAVE


C:\>
```

Note

Some files (especially program files) contain characters that DOS cannot display. You may hear beeps and see strange characters on-screen if you display this type of file. Press Ctrl-C to stop the display.

REVIEW

1 Change to the directory that contains the file you want to display.

2 Type **TYPE**, followed by the complete file name (file name and extension) you want to display.

3 Press **Enter**.

Note

If you see the message File not found, you probably typed the file name incorrectly. Try again. Be sure to type the complete file name, including the extension.

Copy a file

```
C:\>COPY AUTOEXEC.BAT AUTOEXEC.OLD
```

Oops!

If you see the message File cannot be copied onto itself, you either left off the name for the new file or typed the same name for the new file as the original file. You must type the current file name and the name of the copy. Try the command again.

1 **Type CD\ and press Enter.**
This step changes to the root directory. For help with this step, see *TASK: Change to the root directory*.

2 **Type COPY.**
The COPY command tells DOS to make a copy of the file.

3 **Press the space bar once.**
Pressing the space bar once inserts a space between the command name and the next part of the command (the file name).

4 **Type AUTOEXEC.BAT.**
AUTOEXEC.BAT is the name of the file you want to copy.

5 **Press the space bar once.**
Pressing the space bar once inserts a space between the file name and the next part of the command (the file name for the new file).

6 **Type AUTOEXEC.OLD.**
AUTOEXEC.OLD is the name you want to assign the copy of the file. The total command is COPY AUTOEXEC.BAT AUTOEXEC.OLD. This command makes a copy of the file AUTOEXEC.BAT and names the file AUTOEXEC.OLD.

7 **Press Enter.**
Pressing Enter confirms the command. You see the message 1 file(s) copied. Now you have two versions of the same file.

After

```
C:\>COPY AUTOEXEC.BAT AUTOEXEC.OLD
        1 file(s) copied

C:\>DIR AUTOEXEC.*

 Volume in drive C is HARD DISK
 Volume Serial Number is 1724-0637
 Directory of C:\

AUTOEXEC OLD          98 09-04-91  12:49a
AUTOEXEC BAT          98 09-04-91  12:49a
        2 file(s)         196 bytes
                     2367488 bytes free

C:\>
```

Each has a different name. To confirm that a copy has been made, follow the next step.

8 **Type DIR AUTOEXEC.* and press Enter.**
This command tells DOS to display all files with the file name AUTOEXEC and with any extension. You should see both AUTOEXEC.BAT and AUTOEXEC.OLD.

REVIEW

1 Change to the directory that contains the file.

2 Type **COPY**.

3 Press the **space bar once**.

4 Type the name of the file you want to copy.

5 Press the **space bar once**.

6 Type the name of the file for the copy. If necessary, first type the path, the drive letter, or both.

7 Press **Enter**.

Note

To copy a file to another directory, see *TASK: Copy a file to another directory*.

Copy a file to another directory

```
C:\>CD\

C:\>COPY AUTOEXEC.OLD C:\DATA
```

Oops!

If you see the message File not found, the file name could not be found. Be sure you are in the correct directory (the directory that contains the file). Then try the command again.

1 Type **CD\ and press Enter.**
This step changes to the root directory. For help with this step, see *TASK: Change to the root directory*.

2 Type **COPY.**
The COPY command tells DOS to make a copy of the file.

3 Press the **space bar once.**
Pressing the space bar once inserts a space between the command name and the next part of the command.

4 Type **AUTOEXEC.OLD.**
AUTOEXEC.OLD is the name of the file you want to copy. If you don't have a file by this name, type the name of a file that you do have.

5 Press the **space bar once.**
Pressing the space bar once inserts a space between the file name and the next part of the command (the directory for the new file).

6 Type **C:\DATA.**
Typing C:\DATA tells DOS to place the copy in the directory C:\DATA. The file will have the same name.

After

```
C:\>CD\

C:\>COPY AUTOEXEC.OLD C:\DATA
        1 file(s) copied

C:\>CD\DATA

C:\DATA>DIR

 Volume in drive C is HARD DISK
 Volume Serial Number is 1724-0637
 Directory of C:\DATA

.             <DIR>     09-04-91  12:39a
..            <DIR>     09-04-91  12:39a
AUTOEXEC OLD         98 09-04-91  12:49a
        3 file(s)           98 bytes
                      2326528 bytes free

C:\DATA>
```

 Press Enter.
Pressing Enter confirms the command. You see the message
1 file(s) copied. Now you have two versions of the same file: one
in the root directory and one in the DATA directory. Both files have
the same name. (Note in the After screen that the DIR command
was used so that you can see the two copies of the file.)

REVIEW

1 Change to the directory that contains the file you want to copy.

2 Type **COPY**.

3 Press the **space bar once.**

4 Type the name of the file you want to copy.

5 Press the **space bar once.**

6 Type the path—the directory where you want to store the copy. If
you want to name the file something different from the original
name, type the path and the new file name.

7 Press **Enter.**

Note

You can name the file
something different by
typing the new file
name after the path
(step 6 in the TASK
section).

Copy a group of files to another directory

```
C:\>COPY *.BAT C:\DATA
```

1 **From the root directory, type COPY.**
The COPY command tells DOS to make a copy of the file.

2 **Press the space bar once.**
Pressing the space bar once inserts a space between the command name and the next part of the command (the file name).

3 **Type *.BAT.**
After the COPY command, you type the name of the file you want to copy. In this case, you tell DOS to copy a group of files. The files can have any file name, but they must have the extension BAT.

4 **Press the space bar once.**
Pressing the space bar once inserts a space between the file name and the next part of the command (the path for the new files).

5 **Type C:\DATA.**
C:\DATA is the path name. This command tells DOS to copy all files with a BAT extension to the directory DATA. (You may have just one file with this extension.) The files will have the same name.

6 **Press Enter.**
Pressing Enter confirms the command. Now you have two versions of each BAT file: one in the original directory and one in the new directory (DATA).

After

```
C:\>COPY *.BAT C:\DATA
AUTOEXEC.BAT
Q.BAT
WS4.BAT
        3 file(s) copied

C:\>
```

Note

Use these same steps to copy a group of files to another drive. To do so, type the new drive name for step 5 in the Task section (for example, **A:**). You don't have to type the file name. If you leave off the file name, DOS uses the same name for the files.

REVIEW

1 Type **COPY**.

2 Press the **space bar once**.

3 Type the name of the files you want to copy. Use the asterisk wild card (*) to match any characters. Use the question mark wild card (?) to match a single character.

4 Press the **space bar once**.

5 Type the name of the directory in which you want to place the files.

6 Press **Enter**.

Note

Be sure to type a directory name. If the directory does not exist or is typed incorrectly, DOS adds all the files together and places them in another file. If you type **DAT**, for example, all files are placed in a file (not directory) named DAT.

Copy all files to a different drive

```
C:\>CD\DATA

C:\DATA>COPY *.* A:
```

1 **Insert a formatted disk into drive A.**
For help with this step, see *TASK: Insert a disk*.

2 **Type CD\DATA.**
Typing this command tells DOS to switch to the DATA directory.

3 **Press Enter.**
Pressing Enter confirms the command. The current directory is now DATA.

4 **Type COPY.**
COPY is the copy command. It tells DOS to copy files.

5 **Press the space bar once.**
Pressing the space bar once inserts a space between the command name and the next part of the command (the files to copy).

6 **Type *.*.**
After the COPY command, you type the name of the file you want to copy. In this case, you tell DOS to copy all files (*.* matches all files).

7 **Press the space bar once.**
The space bar inserts a space between the file name and the next part of the command (the destination for the files).

After

```
C:\>CD\DATA

C:\DATA>COPY *.* A:
AUTOEXEC.OLD
AUTOEXEC.BAT
Q.BAT
WS4.BAT
        4 file(s) copied

C:\DATA>A:

A:\>DIR

 Volume in drive A is DATA DISK
 Volume Serial Number is 07E9-1C5B
 Directory of A:\

AUTOEXEC OLD         98 09-04-91  12:49a
AUTOEXEC BAT         98 09-04-91  12:49a
Q        BAT        128 08-28-91  12:01a
WS4      BAT        128 08-28-91  12:02a
        4 file(s)        452 bytes
                      726016 bytes free

A:\>
```

 Type A:.
A: is the drive name for drive A. This command tells DOS to copy all files to drive A. The files will have the same name.

 Press Enter.
Pressing Enter confirms the command. Now you have two versions of each file: one in the original directory (DATA) and one on drive A.

 Type A: and press Enter.
This step makes drive A the current drive.

11 **Type DIR and press Enter.**
This step displays a directory listing of the contents of the disk in drive A so that you can verify that the copies were made.

REVIEW

 Insert a floppy disk into the drive.

 Change to the directory that contains the files you want to copy.

 Type COPY *.* A:. If you want to specify a different drive, type that drive name instead of A:.

4 Press Enter.

Note

Use the same procedure to copy files from drive A to drive C. Start from drive A and then type **COPY *.* C:**.

Rename a file

C:\DATA>RENAME AUTOEXEC.OLD AUTOEXEC.BAK

Oops!

If you see the message Duplicate file name or file not found, the new name you typed already exists or the original name did not exist. Try the command again.

1 **Type CD\DATA and press Enter.**
This command tells DOS to change to the DATA directory. This directory contains the file you want to rename.

2 **Type RENAME.**
You use the RENAME command to rename files.

3 **Press the space bar once.**
Pressing the space bar once inserts a space between the command name and the next part of the command (the name of the file you want to rename).

4 **Type AUTOEXEC.OLD.**
AUTOEXEC.OLD is the name of the file you want to rename. If you do not have this file, type the name of one you do have.

5 **Press the space bar once.**
Pressing the space bar once inserts a space between the file name and the next part of the command (the new name you want to assign the file).

6 **Type AUTOEXEC.BAK.**
AUTOEXEC.BAK is the new name you want to assign the file.

7 **Press Enter.**
Pressing Enter confirms the command. The file named AUTOEXEC.OLD is now named AUTOEXEC.BAK.

After

```
C:\DATA>RENAME AUTOEXEC.OLD AUTOEXEC.BAK

C:\DATA>DIR

 Volume in drive C is HARD DISK
 Volume Serial Number is 1724-0637
 Directory of C:\DATA

.            <DIR>      09-04-91  12:39a
..           <DIR>      09-04-91  12:39a
AUTOEXEC BAK         98 09-04-91  12:49a
AUTOEXEC BAT         98 09-04-91  12:49a
Q        BAT        128 08-28-91  12:01a
WS4      BAT        128 08-28-91  12:02a
        6 file(s)          452 bytes
                       2220032 bytes free

C:\DATA>
```

8 **Type DIR and press Enter.**
This step displays a directory listing so that you can verify the file
was renamed.

REVIEW

1 Change to the directory that contains the file you want to rename.

2 Type **RENAME**.

3 Press the **space bar once**.

4 Type the name of the file you want to rename. (You can use wild
cards to specify a group of files.)

5 Press the **space bar once**.

6 Type the new name you want to assign the file. (If you specified a
group of files for step 4, you can use wild cards to specify the new
name of a group of files.)

7 Press **Enter**.

Note

You also can rename a
group of files. For step
4 of the Task section,
use wild cards to
specify the files you
want to rename. For
step 6 of the Task
section, use wild cards
to specify the names
for the new files. For
instance, RENAME
*.DOC.TXT renames
all files with a DOC
extension to files with
TXT extension.

Delete a file

C:\DATA>DEL AUTOEXEC.BAK

Oops!

If you see the message File not found, the file name that you typed does not exist. Check your typing and try again.

 Type CD\DATA and press Enter.
This step tells DOS to change to the DATA directory. This directory contains the file you want to rename.

2 **Type DEL.**
The DEL command tells DOS to delete a file.

3 **Press the space bar once.**
Pressing the space bar once inserts a space between the command name and the next part of the command (the file name).

4 **Type AUTOEXEC.BAK.**
AUTOEXEC.BAK is the name of the file you want to delete. If you don't have a file named AUTOEXEC.BAK, type the name of one that you do have. Be sure, however, that you want to delete the file.

5 **Press Enter.**
Pressing Enter confirms the command. The file you specified is deleted.

6 **Type DIR and press Enter.**
This step displays a directory listing so that you can verify the file was deleted.

After

```
C:\DATA>DEL AUTOEXEC.BAK

C:\DATA>DIR

 Volume in drive C is HARD DISK
 Volume Serial Number is 1724-0637
 Directory of C:\DATA

.            <DIR>     09-04-91  12:39a
..           <DIR>     09-04-91  12:39a
AUTOEXEC BAT       98  09-04-91  12:49a
Q        BAT      128  08-28-91  12:01a
WS4      BAT      128  08-28-91  12:02a
        5 file(s)        354 bytes
                     2195456 bytes free

C:\DATA>
```

Note

You can delete a group of files by using wild cards for the file name in step 4 of the TASK section. To delete all files, see *TASK: Delete all files*.

REVIEW

1 Change to the directory that contains the file you want to delete.

2 Type **DEL**.

3 Press the **space bar once**.

4 Type the name of the file you want to delete.

5 Press **Enter**.

Note

It's easy to type **DEL** when you mean to type something else. Be sure to read all prompts carefully. Also, it's good practice to use the DIR command to review the file listing of the disk or directory before you delete all the files.

Delete all files

```
A:\>DEL *.*
All files in directory will be deleted!
Are you sure (Y/N)?
```

Oops!

If you change your mind, type N in step 7 of the TASK section.

1 **Insert a disk into drive A.**
Use the disk that you have used for other tasks. If you haven't been following other tasks, insert a disk that contains files you do not need. Don't insert a disk with files you want to save.

If you need help inserting the disk, see *TASK: Insert a disk*.

2 **Type A: and press Enter.**
This step tells DOS to switch to drive A. Drive A contains the files you want to delete.

To delete files in a directory, change to that directory.

3 **Type DEL.**
The DEL command tells DOS to delete a file.

4 **Press the space bar once.**
Pressing the space bar once inserts a space between the command name and the next part of the command (the file name).

5 **Type *.*.**
After the DEL command, you type the name of the file you want to delete. The wild cards used here (*.*) specify all files.

Be sure that you want to delete all files.

After

```
A:\>DEL *.*
All files in directory will be deleted!
Are you sure (Y/N)?Y

A:\>DIR

 Volume in drive A is DATA DISK
 Volume Serial Number is 07E9-1C5B
 Directory of A:\

File not found

A:\>
```

 Press Enter.
Pressing Enter confirms the command. You see the message
`All files in directory will be deleted! Are you sure (Y/N)?`

 Type Y.
Typing Y confirms the deletion. All files are deleted.

 Type DIR and press Enter.
This step displays a directory listing so that you can confirm that the
files were deleted.

REVIEW

 Change to the drive or directory that contains the files you want to
delete.

2 Type **DEL**.

3 Press the **space bar once**.

4 Type *.* and press **Enter**.

5 Type **Y**.

Undelete a file

```
A:\>UNDELETE
```

Oops!

Not all files can be deleted. See *Using MS-DOS 6.2,* Special Edition, for more information on how DOS deletes and undeletes files.

 Insert a disk into drive A.
Use the disk that you have used for other tasks. If you haven't been following other tasks, insert a disk that contains files that have been deleted.

 Type A: and press Enter.
This step tells DOS to switch to drive A. Drive A contains the files you want to undelete.

To undelete files in a directory, change to that directory for this step.

 Type UNDELETE and press Enter.
This command undeletes files and is only available with DOS 5, 6, and 6.2. You see some information on-screen:

>   Directory used
>
>   File specifications
>
>   Status of deletion tracking file
>
>   Number of files deleted
>
>   Number of files able to be recovered

After this information, you see the first deleted file that DOS found. The file name, extension, size, date, and time are listed. The first character of the file name is replaced with a question mark.

After

```
Using the MS-DOS directory.

    ?UTOEXEC OLD        98  9-04-91 12:49a  ...A  Undelete (Y/N)?Y
    Please type the first character for ?UTOEXEC.OLD: A

File successfully undeleted.

    ?UTOEXEC BAT        98  9-04-91 12:49a  ...A  Undelete (Y/N)?Y
    Please type the first character for ?UTOEXEC.BAT: A

File successfully undeleted.

    ?        BAT       128  8-28-91 12:01a  ...A  Undelete (Y/N)?Y
    Please type the first character for ?        .BAT: Q

File successfully undeleted.

    ?S4      BAT       128  8-28-91 12:02a  ...A  Undelete (Y/N)?Y
    Please type the first character for ?S4      .BAT: W

File successfully undeleted.



A:\>
```

Following the file information is the prompt Undelete (Y/N)?

 Type Y.
This step tells DOS to undelete this file. You see the message Please type the first character for ?UTOEXEC.BAT.

 Type A.
A is the first character of this file name. The file is undeleted, and you return to the DOS prompt. (If other files were deleted, you can undelete this also. Type Y to tell DOS to undelete the file; then type the first letter. The After screen shows other files being undeleted.)

REVIEW

 Change to the drive or directory that contains the file or files you want to undelete.

 Type **UNDELETE**.

 Press **Enter**.

 When the file you want to undelete is listed, type **Y**.

 Type the first character of the file name.

6 Continue typing **Y** and the first character of the file name until all files are undeleted.

> **Note**
>
> The UNDELETE command is only available with DOS Versions 5, 6, and 6.2.

> **Note**
>
> If you don't know the first letter of the file, assign any letter. Then after you see what the file contains, use the RENAME command to rename the file.

Undelete a File **101**

Protecting Your Files

This section includes the following tasks:

- Start the Microsoft Backup program

- Configure the Microsoft Backup program

- Back up selected directories

- Back up selected files

- Restore files

- Exit the Microsoft Backup program

- Scan for viruses

- Tell DOS to scan for viruses automatically

Start the Microsoft Backup program

```
C:\>msbackup
```

Oops!

To exit the Microsoft Backup program, see *TASK: Exit the Microsoft Backup program.*

1 **Type MSBACKUP.**
This command starts the Microsoft Backup program. This program enables you to back up your entire disk or select only certain directories or files to back up. You also can control the backup method.

For complete information on the Microsoft Backup program, see *Using MS-DOS 6.2,* Special Edition.

2 **Press Enter.**
If you are running the program for the first time, you are prompted to select the configuration. (For more information about selecting the configuration, see *TASK: Configure the Microsoft Backup program.*)

If you have already configured the program, the main menu appears. You can choose to Backup, Restore, or Compare files.

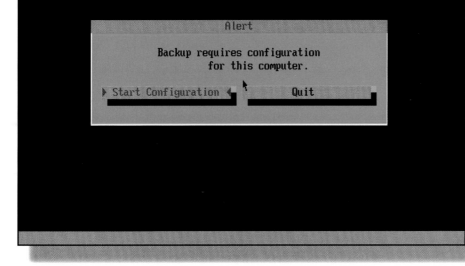

REVIEW

1 Type **MSBACKUP**.

2 Press **Enter**.

DOS 6 and 6.2 include a Microsoft Windows version of the Backup program. See *Using MS-DOS 6.2,* Special Edition for help on this program.

The MSBACKUP command is only available with DOS 6 and 6.2.

Note

A *backup* is an extra set of the data and programs on your hard disk. If something happens to the original copy, you can use the backup to restore the data and programs.

Configure the Microsoft Backup program

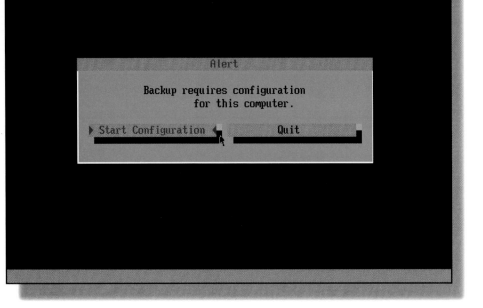

(Part 1 of 3)
This task consists of three parts. The first part, Start the configuration, is covered here. The next four pages explain the rest of the task.

Oops!

If you don't want to do the configuration, select the Quit option. You can run the configuration program later. Until you complete the configuration, every time you use Microsoft Backup, DOS will remind you that you need to run the Floppy Drive Change Line Test.

1 **When the alert box tells you that Microsoft Backup requires configuration, press Enter.**
This alert box appears the first time you run Microsoft Backup. Pressing Enter selects the Start Configuration option. You see options for the screen display and mouse. Microsoft Backup tries to determine the type of mouse and monitor you are using; generally the program guesses correctly.

2 **Press Enter.**
This step accepts the defaults for the screen and mouse options. You are next prompted to perform the Floppy Drive Change Line Test. Performing this test ensures that Microsoft Backup can use the fastest and most reliable method of backing up.

3 **Press Enter.**
This step starts the floppy drive test. The next screen lists the backup devices.

4 **Press Enter.**
This step accepts the default backup devices. Microsoft Backup tests the CPU speed, reads the hard drive, and displays a performance index. You are next prompted for a Floppy Disk Compatibility Test.

Turn the page to continue configuring Microsoft Backup.

After

```
┌─┐  ┌─┐                Floppy Disk Compatibility Test
│─│  │─│
│    │    The compatibility test consists of a small backup and
│    │    compare, automatically performed by Backup.
│
│id        You will see the dialog boxes opened and the selections
│ 2        automatically made.  The only selection you must make
│          is the floppy disk drive to use for the test.  You will
│          see a message telling you when to make this selection.
│
│ac        The compatibility test is important, because it verifies
│ A        that Backup is configured correctly for your
│          computer, and that you will be able to make reliable
│          backups.
│
│          You will need two floppy disks of the same type for
│          this test.
│
│
│              ▶ Start Test ◀    Skip Test    Cancel
│
│
Go ahead with the compatibility test                    Waiting
```

REVIEW

1 When the Alert box appears, press **Enter** to start the configuration.

2 Change any screen display and mouse options; then press **Enter**.

3 Press **Enter** to start the floppy drive test.

4 Press **Enter** to accept the default backup devices.

Configure the Microsoft Backup program

(Part 2 of 3)
This task consists of three parts. The first part, Configure the Microsoft Backup program, is covered on the preceding two pages. These two pages cover the second part. Turn the page for the conclusion of this task.

Oops!

To skip the test, select Skip Test for step 1.

Floppy Disk Compatibility Test

The compatibility test consists of a small backup and compare, automatically performed by Backup.

You will see the dialog boxes opened and the selections automatically made. The only selection you must make is the floppy disk drive to use for the test. You will see a message telling you when to make this selection.

The compatibility test is important, because it verifies that Backup is configured correctly for your computer, and that you will be able to make reliable backups.

You will need two floppy disks of the same type for this test.

  ► Start Test ◄   Skip Test   Cancel

Go ahead with the compatibility test   Waiting

1 **When DOS asks you whether you want to run the compatibility test, press Enter.**
This step starts the test. The Microsoft Backup program goes through a backup routine, selecting the appropriate options and test files. You see a message stating that the test will be paused so that you can select the backup device.

2 **Press Enter.**
This step clears the message.

DOS prompts you to select the device (floppy drive) that you want to back up to. The default, drive A, is selected.

3 **Press Enter.**
This step accepts the default drive—drive A—as the device that you will back up to. DOS then prompts you to insert a floppy disk.

4 **Insert a floppy disk and press Enter.**
Be sure that you insert a blank disk. If you insert a disk that contains information, the information will be overwritten. (DOS does warn you, however, before overwriting the information.)

The backup process begins. When the first disk you inserted is filled with information, DOS prompts you to insert another disk.

After

```
                Disk Backup Compatibility Test 2.10.07a

                            ┌─────── Alert ───────┐
                            │                     │
                    Insert diskette # 1 into drive A.
                            │                     │
                    ┌──────────────┐   ┌──────────────────┐
                  ▶ │   Continue   │ ◀ │   Cancel Backup  │
                    └──────────────┘   └──────────────────┘

      ┌─── Diskette Progress ───┐   ┌─── Backup Set Information ───┐
  Drive A:                        Catalog: CC30119A Type  : Full
  Track :                         Name   : CONFID$$ Verify: Rd Compare

  Drive B:                        Estimated              Actual
  Track :                         ─────────────────────────────────
                                         2  ◀ Disks ▶
  Your Time  :  0:00  % Complete:    %    19  ◀ Files ▶
  Backup Time:  0:00  DOS Index :    %  1,368,646  ◀ Bytes ▶
  Compression:        Kbytes/Min:        1:27  ◀ Time  ▶      0:00
```

REVIEW

1 Press **Enter** to start the test.

2 Press **Enter** to continue.

3 Press **Enter** to accept the default drive.

4 Insert the first disk and press **Enter**.

Note

If you receive any error messages, see *Using MS-DOS 6.2,* Special Edition, for help.

Configure the Microsoft Backup program

(Part 3 of 3)
This task consists of three parts. The preceding four pages explained the beginning of the process. These two pages conclude the process.

Oops!

If you accidentally insert a disk that contains information you want to save, eject the disk, insert another disk, and press Enter.

```
              Disk Backup Compatibility Test 2.10.07a

┌─────────────────────────── Alert ───────────────────────────┐
│                                                              │
│          Insert diskette # 1 into drive A.                   │
│                                                              │
│   ▶ Continue  ◀        Cancel Backup                         │
└──────────────────────────────────────────────────────────────┘

     Diskette Progress              Backup Set Information
  Drive A:                      Catalog: CC30119A Type  : Full
  Track  :                      Name    : CONFID$$ Verify: Rd Compare

  Drive B:                         Estimated           Actual
  Track  :
                                        2  ◀ Disks ▶
  Your Time  :  0:00  % Complete:  %     19  ◀ Files ▶
  Backup Time:  0:00  DOS Index :  %  1,368,646  ◀ Bytes ▶
  Compression:        Kbytes/Min:        1:27  ◀ Time  ▶       0:00
```

 Eject the first disk, insert another disk, and press Enter.
This step continues the backup process. You see the progress of the backup on-screen. A message appears telling you that the backup is complete.

 Press Enter.
This step clears the message and starts the compare process. (The *compare process* compares the backup information to the original information to make sure that the backup copy is accurate.) You are prompted to insert disk 1.

3 **Insert disk 1 and press Enter.**
The compare process starts. DOS then prompts you to insert disk 2.

4 **Insert disk 2 and press Enter.**
You see a message that says the compare process is complete.

5 **Press Enter.**
You see a message that says the test was successful.

 Press Enter.
This step saves the configuration and returns you to the main menu.

After

```
┌─┐                    Microsoft Backup                          ┐
│─│
│   File      Help                                               │
│                                                                │
│                                                                │
│          ┌─┐              Backup 2.09.14                 ┐     │
│          │─│                                             │     │
│          │                                               │     │
│          │    ┌──────────────┐       ┌──────────────┐    │     │
│          │    │    Backup     │     ▷│   Restore    │◁   │     │
│          │    └──────────────┘       └──────────────┘    │     │
│          │                                               │     │
│          │    ┌──────────────┐       ┌──────────────┐    │     │
│          │    │   Compare    │       │  Configure   │    │     │
│          │    └──────────────┘       └──────────────┘    │     │
│          │                                               │     │
│          │          ┌──────────────┐                     │     │
│          │          │     Quit     │  ▶                  │     │
│          │          └──────────────┘                     │     │
│          │                                               │     │
│          └───────────────────────────────────────────────┘     │
│                                                                │
│                                                                │
│   Restore files to your hard disk or network drive            │
└────────────────────────────────────────────────────────────────┘
```

REVIEW

1 Eject the first disk, insert the second disk, and press **Enter**.

2 Press **Enter** to start the compare.

3 Insert disk 1 and press **Enter**.

4 Insert disk 2 and press **Enter**.

5 Press **Enter** to end the compare.

6 Press **Enter** to return to the main menu.

> **Note**
>
> If you configured the program previously but did not run the test, you can run the test at any time. To do so, select Configure from the main menu. Then select Compatibility test and run the test.

Back up selected directories

```
C:\>
```

(Part 1 of 2)
Backing up selected directories is a two-part process. These two pages cover the first part. Turn the page for the second part.

Oops!

To return to the Backup screen, click on the Cancel button.

1 **Start the Microsoft Backup program.**
For help with this task, see *TASK: Start the Microsoft Backup program*.

2 **From the main menu, press Enter.**
Pressing Enter selects the first choice on the main menu, Backup, which is highlighted. You see the Backup screen. Certain options are preset, depending on your configuration. By default, the default set is used, drive C is the drive to be backed up, drive A is the drive to back up to, and the full method is used.

3 **Type 1.**
This step selects the Select Files option. You have to specify the files to back up. You see a directory listing on the left side of the screen and a file listing on the right.

After

```
┌─┬──────────────── Select Backup Files ─────────────────┬─┐
│ [-C-] [-F-]                                               │
│ ─────────────────────────────────────────────────────── │
│ C:\*.*                                                    │
│ ───────────────────────────────────────────────────────  │
│ ┌C:\         ┐▲│ autoexec.bak    299   8-18-92  1:04p ...a│▲│
│  ─123R24       │ autoexec.bat    342  12-03-92  3:32p ...a│ │
│     └WYSIWYG   │ autoexec.old    313   9-14-92  8:22a ....│ │
│  ─AFTERDRK     │ befsetup.msd 65,411  12-03-92  3:21p ...a│ │
│     ─ADMODULE.SDK│ chklist .ms     162  10-21-92  9:19a ...a│ │
│        └BLANKER  │ command .com 53,022 10-26-92  6:00a ...a│ │
│     ─BITMAPS   │ config  .sys    275  12-03-92  3:32p ...a│ │
│  ─ALDUS        │ dialog1 .xlm 28,347   9-28-92  7:48a ...a│ │
│     └USENGLSH  │ dsvxd   .386  5,741  10-26-92  6:00a ...a│ │
│        ─FILTERS│ fontwid .bat     50   7-26-90  2:06p ...a│ │
│        └SETUP ▼│ himem   .sys 11,304   5-01-90  3:00a ...a│▼│
│ ─────────────────────────────────────────────────────── │
│ Total Files: 4,661 [   182,522 K]  Selected Files:    1 [       8 K] │
│ ─────────────────────────────────────────────────────── │
│ ┌ Include ┐ ┌ Exclude ┐ ┌ Special ┐  ┌ Display ┐ ► OK ◄ ┌ Cancel ┐ │
│ ─────────────────────────────────────────────────────── │
│ Select entire directories with right mouse button or Spacebar │
└───────────────────────────────────────────────────────────┘
```

REVIEW

1 Start the Microsoft Backup program.

2 From the main menu, select **Backup**.

3 Type 1 to select Select Files.

Note

For more information on the backup process, see *Using MS-DOS 6.2,* Special Edition.

Back up selected directories

(Part 2 of 2)
Backing up selected directories is a two-part process. The preceding two pages cover the first part. These two pages cover the second part.

```
                    Select Backup Files
[-C-] [-F-]
─────────────────────────────────────────────────────
C:\*.*

┌─C:\─────────────────┐  ┌─ autoexec.bak    299    8-18-92   1:04p  ...a ─┐
│ ┌─123R24           │  │  autoexec.bat    342   12-03-92   3:32p  ...a  │
│ │  └─WYSIWYG        │  │  autoexec.old    313    9-14-92   8:22a  .... │
│ ├─AFTERDRK          │  │  befsetup.msd 65,411   12-03-92   3:21p  ...a │
│ │  ├─ADMODULE.SDK   │  │  chklist .ms     162   10-21-92   9:19a  ...a │
│ │  │  └─BLANKER     │  │  command .com 53,022   10-26-92   6:00a  ...a │
│ │  └─BITMAPS        │  │  config  .sys    275   12-03-92   3:32p  ...a │
│ ├─ALDUS             │  │  dialog1 .xlm 28,347    9-28-92   7:48a  ...a │
│ │  └─USENGLSH       │  │  dsvxd   .386  5,741   10-26-92   6:00a  ...a │
│ │    ├─FILTERS      │  │  fontwid .bat     50    7-26-90   2:06p  ...a │
│ │    └─SETUP        │  └  himem   .sys 11,304    5-01-90   3:00a  ...a ┘
└─────────────────────┘
─────────────────────────────────────────────────────
Total Files:  4,661 [  182,522 K]   Selected Files:     1 [      8 K]

 [ Include ]  [ Exclude ]  [ Special ]   [ Display ] ► [ OK ] ◄ [ Cancel ]

Select entire directories with right mouse button or Spacebar
```

Oops!

To cancel the backup, select Cancel before step 5 in the TASK section.

 Press the ↓ key to highlight the DATA directory.
This step selects the directory that you want to back up. If you don't have this directory, select one you do have.

 Press the space bar.
This step marks the directory to be backed up. The directory has an arrow next to it, and all files in the file list have a check mark next to them. These symbols indicate that the directory and all files are selected.

3 Press Enter.
This step confirms your backup selections and returns you to the Backup screen. Microsoft Backup calculates the number of disks you will need and the total size of all selected files.

 Type S.
This step selects the Start Backup button. You are prompted to insert a disk.

 Insert the disk and press Enter.
You may be prompted to insert additional disks. If so, insert the disk and press Enter. When all files have been backed up, you see a message that reads Backup Complete. The After screen shows this step.

After

```
                        Backup 2.09.14
  C:\DOS
                     ┌─ Backup Complete ──────────┐
      ┌─WPC          │ Selected  files:      4    │    5,472  12-04-92
      ├─WPWIN        │ Backed up files:      4    │
      │   ├─GRAPHICS │ Skipped:              0    │
      │   ├─LEARN    │                            │
      │   └─MACROS   │ Disks:                1    │
      └─WS4          │ Bytes:           67,268    │
  C:\               │                             │
      └─»DOS         │ Total Time:        0:07    │
                     │ Your Time:   ▶    0:02     │
         Diskette Prog│ Backup Time:      0:05    │   Set Information
                     │                            │
  Drive A:     [▬▬   │ KBytes Per Min:    804     │ 04B Type  : Full
  Track  :  5        │ Compression:       1.6     │ LT  Verify: Off
                     │                            │
  Drive B:           │                            │        Actual
  Track  :           │      ▶   OK   ◀            │
                     └────────────────────────────┘ Disks ▶        1
  Your Time  :  0:02   % C                        ◀ Files ▶        4
  Backup Time:  0:05   DOS Index  :  100%    67,268 ◀ Bytes ▶  67,268
  Compression:  1.6    Kbytes/Min:  804     0:15 ◀ Time ▶    0:07
```

 Press Enter.

This step returns you to the main menu. To exit the Microsoft
Backup program, see *TASK: Exit the Microsoft Backup program*.

REVIEW

1 Highlight the first directory you want to back up.

2 Press the **space bar**.

3 Repeat steps 4 and 5 for all directories you want to back up.

4 Press **Enter** when you finish selecting directories.

5 Type **S** to start the backup.

6 Insert disks and press **Enter** as prompted.

> **Note**
>
> Clearly label the
> disks that you use in
> numerical order—for
> example, Backup disk
> 1, Backup disk 2, and
> so on. You will need to
> restore the information
> in the same order you
> backed it up.

> **Note**
>
> See *TASK: Restore
> files* for help restoring
> backup files.

Back up selected files

(Part 1 of 2)
Backing up selected files is a two-part process. These two pages cover the first part of the process. Turn the page for the second part.

 Oops!

To return to the Backup screen, click on the Cancel button.

1 **Start the Microsoft Backup program.**
For help with this task, see *TASK: Start the Microsoft Backup program*.

2 **From the Main menu, press Enter.**
By default the first choice, Backup, is selected. Pressing Enter selects this option. You see the Backup screen. Certain options are preset, depending on your configuration. By default, the default set is used, drive C is the drive to be backed up, drive A is the drive to back up to, and the full method is used.

3 **Type 1.**
This step selects the Select Files option. You have to specify the files to back up. You see a directory listing on the left of the screen and a file listing on the right.

After

```
┌─────────────────────────────────────────────────────────┐
│─                    Select Backup Files                  │
│ [-C-]  [-F-]                                             │
│ ─────────────────────────────────────────────────────── │
│ C:\*.*                                                   │
│ ─────────────────────────────────────────────────────── │
│ C:\            ↑│ autoexec.bak    299    8-18-92   1:04p ...a ◄↑│
│   ─123R24       │ autoexec.bat    342   12-03-92   3:32p ...a  │
│     └─WYSIWYG   │ autoexec.old    313    9-14-92   8:22a ....  │
│   ─AFTERDRK     │ befsetup.msd  65,411  12-03-92   3:21p ...a  │
│     ├─ADMODULE.SDK│ chklist .ms     162  10-21-92   9:19a ...a │
│     │ └─BLANKER │ command .com  53,022  10-26-92   6:00a ...a  │
│     └─BITMAPS   │ config  .sys    275   12-03-92   3:32p ...a  │
│   ─ALDUS        │ dialog1 .xlm  28,347   9-28-92   7:48a ...a  │
│     └─USENGLSH  │ dsvxd   .386   5,741  10-26-92   6:00a ...a  │
│       ├─FILTERS │ fontwid .bat     50    7-26-90   2:06p ...a  │
│       └─SETUP  ↓│ himem   .sys  11,304   5-01-90   3:00a ...a ↓│
│ ─────────────────────────────────────────────────────── │
│ Total Files:  4,661 [   182,522 K]   Selected Files:  3 [    60 K]│
│ ─────────────────────────────────────────────────────── │
│ ┌─Include─┐ ┌─Exclude─┐ ┌─Special─┐ ┌─Display─┐ ► OK ◄ ┌─Cancel─┐│
│                                                          │
│ Select entire directories with right mouse button or Spacebar│
└─────────────────────────────────────────────────────────┘
```

REVIEW

 Start the Microsoft Backup program.

 From the main menu, select Backup.

3 Type **1** to select Select Files.

Note

See *TASK: Restore files* for help restoring the backup files.

Back up selected files

(Part 2 of 2)
Backing up selected directories is a two-part process. The preceding two pages cover the first part. These two pages cover the second part.

Oops!

To cancel the backup, select Cancel before step 7 of the Task section.

```
                    Select Backup Files
[-C-]  [-F-]

C:\*.*

C:\                      autoexec.bak    299    8-18-92   1:04p  ...a
─123R24                  autoexec.bat    342   12-03-92   3:32p  ...a
  └─WYSIWYG              autoexec.old    313    9-14-92   8:22a  ....
─AFTERDRK                befsetup.msd  65,411  12-03-92   3:21p  ...a
  ├─ADMODULE.SDK         chklist .ms      162  10-21-92   9:19a  ...a
  │ └─BLANKER            command .com  53,022  10-26-92   6:00a  ...a
  └─BITMAPS              config  .sys     275  12-03-92   3:32p  ...a
─ALDUS                   dialog1 .xlm  28,347   9-28-92   7:48a  ...a
  └─USENGLSH             dsvxd   .386   5,741  10-26-92   6:00a  ...a
    ├─FILTERS            fontwid .bat      50   7-26-90   2:06p  ...a
    └─SETUP              himem   .sys  11,304   5-01-90   3:00a  ...a

Total Files:  4,661 [   182,522 K]   Selected Files:    3 [       60 K]

  Include    Exclude    Special     Display  ▶  OK  ◀   Cancel

Select entire directories with right mouse button or Spacebar
```

 Press the ↓ key to highlight the Excel directory.
This step selects the directory that contains the file you want to back up. The files in this directory appear in the right side of the window. If you have already backed up files, these files might already be selected. To unselect a file or directory, press the space bar to remove the arrow (directory) or check mark (file).

 Press the → key to move to the file listing.
This step moves the cursor to the file listing.

 Press the ↓ key to highlight the BOOKS.XLS file.
This step marks the file to be backed up. If you don't have this file, select one that you do have.

 Press the space bar.
This step places a check mark next to the file. (*Note:* If the file already has a check mark next to it, skip this step.)

 Press Enter.
This step confirms your backup selections and returns you to the backup screen. Microsoft Backup calculates the number of disks you will need and the total size of all selected files.

6 **Type S.**
This step selects the Start Backup button. You are prompted to insert a disk.

After

```
┌─────────────────────────────────────────────────────────┐
│ [-]                  Microsoft Backup                     │
│   File    Help                                            │
│ ┌───────────────────────────────────────────────────┐   │
│ │[-]              Backup 2.09.14                     │   │
│ │                                                    │   │
│ │  ┌─────────────────┐      ┌─────────────────┐      │   │
│ │ ▶│     Backup     ◀│      │     Restore     │      │   │
│ │  └─────────────────┘      └─────────────────┘      │   │
│ │  ┌─────────────────┐      ┌─────────────────┐      │   │
│ │  │    Compare      │      │   Configure     │      │   │
│ │  └─────────────────┘      └─────────────────┘      │   │
│ │             ┌─────────────────┐                    │   │
│ │             │      Quit       │                    │   │
│ │             └─────────────────┘                    │   │
│ │                                                    │   │
│ └───────────────────────────────────────────────────┘   │
│                                                           │
│ Back up your hard disks and network drives               │
└─────────────────────────────────────────────────────────┘
```

7 **Insert the disk and press Enter.**
When all files have been backed up, you see a message that reads
`Backup Complete`.

8 **Press Enter.**
This step returns you to the main menu. To exit the Microsoft
Backup program, see *TASK: Exit the Microsoft Backup program*.

REVIEW

1 Use the ↓ key to highlight the directory that contains the first file
you want to back up.

2 Press the → key to move to the file listing.

3 Use the ↓ key to select the file.

4 Press the **space bar**.

5 Repeat steps 4 through 7 for all directories you want to back up.
Then press **Enter.**

6 Type **S** to start the backup.

7 Insert disks and press **Enter** as prompted.

> **Note**
>
> You can select more
> than one file. Follow
> the same procedure to
> mark all the files you
> want to back up.

> **Note**
>
> If other files were
> selected previously—
> the last time you ran
> Backup—those files
> will be backed up as
> well. To exclude those
> files, deselect them.
> (For information, see
> *Using MS-DOS 6.2,*
> Special Edition.)

Restore files

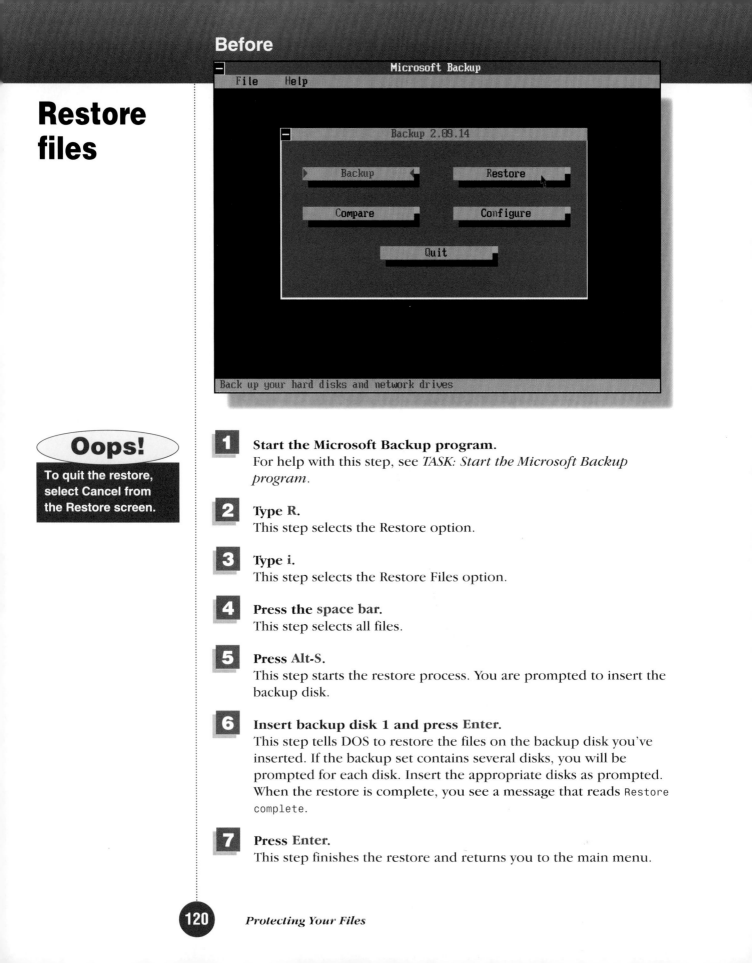

Microsoft Backup

File   Help

Backup 2.09.14

▶ Backup ◀   Restore

Compare   Configure

Quit

Back up your hard disks and network drives

Oops!

To quit the restore, select Cancel from the Restore screen.

1 **Start the Microsoft Backup program.**
For help with this step, see *TASK: Start the Microsoft Backup program*.

2 **Type R.**
This step selects the Restore option.

3 **Type i.**
This step selects the Restore Files option.

4 **Press the space bar.**
This step selects all files.

5 **Press Alt-S.**
This step starts the restore process. You are prompted to insert the backup disk.

6 **Insert backup disk 1 and press Enter.**
This step tells DOS to restore the files on the backup disk you've inserted. If the backup set contains several disks, you will be prompted for each disk. Insert the appropriate disks as prompted. When the restore is complete, you see a message that reads Restore complete.

7 **Press Enter.**
This step finishes the restore and returns you to the main menu.

After

```
                    Restore 2.09.14
 C:\EXCEL
 ┌─────────────────── Restore Complete ───────────────────┐
 │                                                         │
 │    ─MACROS                                 5,712  8-17-92
 │    ─PRINT      Selected files:       1  ▸
 │  ─WPC          Restored files:       1
 │  ─WPWIN        Skipped  files:       0
 │    ─GRAPHICS
 │    ─LEARN      Disks:                1
 │    ─MACROS     Bytes:            5,712
 │  ─WS4
 │                Total Time:        0:04
 │                Your Time:        0:00
 │                Restore Time:     0:04
 │ Drive A:   [      ]                       204F  Overwrite: Always
 │ Track :  10    Errors Found:        0    ULT  Confirm  : No
 │                Errors Corrected:    0
 │ Drive B:       Pauses:              0              Actual
 │ Track :                                    ─────────────────
 │                                         ◄ Disks ►        1
 │ Your Time :  0:00 %  ▸    OK    ◄       ◄ Files ►        1
 │ Restore Time: 0:04 D                    ◄ Bytes ►    5,712
 │ Errors Found:   0  C                    ◄ Time  ►     0:04
 └─────────────────────────────────────────────────────────┘
```

Note

For help on exiting, see *TASK: Exit the Microsoft Backup program.*

Note

Backed up files are stored in a special format that DOS cannot read directly. In order to use those files, you must run them through the restore process, which makes the files readable.

REVIEW

1 Start the Microsoft Backup program.

2 Type **R** to select the Restore option.

3 Type **i** to select the Restore Files option.

4 Press the **space bar** to select all files.

5 Press **Alt-S** to start the restore.

6 Insert the backup disks and press **Enter** as prompted.

7 Press **Enter**.

Exit the Microsoft Backup program

Oops!

If you aren't at the Backup main menu, press Esc until the menu appears.

From the Backup main menu, type Q.
This step selects the Quit command. You return to the DOS prompt.

After

```
C:\>
```

From the Backup main menu, type **Q**.

Note

For help starting the program, see *TASK: Start the Microsoft Backup program*.

Scan for viruses

Oops!

To cancel the virus scan, select Exit for step 3 of the Task section.

1 **Type MSAV.**
This command starts the anti-virus program used to detect and remove viruses. This program is available only with Versions 6 and 6.2 of DOS.

2 **Press Enter.**
This step executes the command. You see the main menu, which contains options that enable you to detect a virus, detect a virus and clean the disk, select a drive, set options, and exit. The Detect option is selected. The Before screen shows this step.

For complete information on all options, see *Using MS-DOS 6.2*, Special Edition.

3 **Press Enter.**
This step selects the Detect option. The anti-virus program scans memory for viruses, and then checks directories and files. (The scan may take some time.) When the scan is complete, you see a report of what was found—what was checked, infected, and cleaned.

4 **Press Enter.**
This step closes the report. You return to the main menu.

5 **Type x.**
This step selects the Exit option. A message appears prompting you to confirm that you want to exit.

After

```
                        Main Menu
                Viruses Detected and Cleaned

                    Checked        Infected        Cleaned

Hard disks    :        1              0              0
Floppy disks  :        0              0              0
Total disks   :        1              0              0

COM Files     :        72             0              0
EXE Files     :        354            0              0
Other Files   :        4266           0              0
Total Files   :        4692           0              0

Scan Time     :      00:03:52

                                              K
M
▶

F1      F2     F3 Stop  F4     F5     F6     F7     F8     F9     F10
```

 Press Enter.

This step closes the anti-virus program. You return to the DOS prompt.

REVIEW

 Type **MSAV**.

2 Press **Enter**.

3 Select the option you want.

4 Press **Enter**.

5 After reading the results, press **Enter**.

6 Type **x**.

7 Press **Enter**.

Note

If the program finds a virus, call a technical support representative for help. Or see *Using MS-DOS 6.2,* Special Edition, for information.

Note

Included with DOS 6 and 6.2 is a Windows version of the anti-virus program. See *Using MS-DOS 6.2,* Special Edition for help using this program.

Tell DOS to scan for viruses automatically

```
C:\>VSAFE
```

Oops!

To unload the program, press the Alt-V key combination, and then press the Alt-U key combination.

1 **Type VSAFE.**
This command loads a terminate-and-stay-resident (TSR) program that checks for viruses. (A TSR is a program that is loaded into memory and stays there. You can then access the program at any time by pressing a special key combination.)

2 **Press Enter.**
This step executes the command. The program is now loaded into memory. A message appears telling you that the installation is complete; you return to the DOS prompt.

The program will do the following:

- Warn you if a virus tries to format the hard disk.

- Check all executable (EXE) files as they are executed.

- Check the boot sector for viruses.

- Protect the boot sector.

After

```
        VSafe (tm)

   Copyright (c) 1991-1992
   Central Point Software, Inc.
      Hotkey:  <Alt><V>


VSafe successfully installed.
VSafe is using 23K of conventional memory,
              23K of XMS memory,
               0K of EMS memory.


C:\>
```

Note

You must run this program every time you turn on the computer. If you want to set up the program so that you don't have to load it every time you turn on the computer, add the VSAFE program to your AUTOEXEC.BAT file. See *Using MS-DOS 6.2,* Special Edition, for help on this task.

REVIEW

 Type **VSAFE**.

 Press **Enter**.

Note

To change the program settings, press Alt-V to access the menu. For information on the settings, see *Using MS-DOS 6.2,* Special Edition.

Customizing and Optimizing Your Computer

This section covers the following tasks:

- Display a volume label

- Change a volume label

- Check the DOS version

- Check disk space and memory

- Set the date

- Set the time

- Set the path

- Check memory information

- Optimize memory

- Defragment a disk

Display a volume label

```
C:\>VOL
```

Oops!

If you see the message Bad command or file name, you typed the command incorrectly. Try again.

 1 **Type VOL.**
VOL is the volume command. *Volume* is another name for *drive*.

2 **Press Enter.**
Pressing Enter confirms the command. You see the volume label (which is the volume name) assigned to the disk. You also see the volume serial number.

After

```
C:\>VOL

Volume in drive C is HARD DISK
Volume Serial Number is 1724-0637

C:\>
```

REVIEW

 Type **VOL**.

 Press **Enter**.

Change a volume label

```
C:\>LABEL
Volume in drive C is HARD DISK
Volume Serial Number is 1724-0637
Volume label (11 characters, ENTER for none)?
```

Oops!

If you decide not to change the volume label, follow this same procedure to change the label back to its original name.

1 **Type LABEL.**
LABEL is the label command. You use this command to change the volume label for the disk.

2 **Press Enter.**
Pressing Enter confirms the command. You see the volume label (which is the name) currently assigned to the disk and the volume serial number. You also see the prompt Volume label (11 characters, ENTER for none)?

3 **Type SEO'S DISK.**
SEO'S DISK is the new volume label you want to use.

4 **Press Enter.**
Pressing Enter confirms the new volume label.

5 **Type VOL and press Enter.**
This step verifies that the volume label has been changed. You see the volume label listed as SEO'S DISK.

After

```
C:\>LABEL
Volume in drive C is HARD DISK
Volume Serial Number is 1724-0637
Volume label (11 characters, ENTER for none)? SEO'S DISK

C:\>VOL

 Volume in drive C is SEO'S DISK
 Volume Serial Number is 1724-0637

C:\>
```

REVIEW

 1 Type **LABEL**.

 2 Press **Enter**.

 3 Type the label (up to 11 characters). You can include spaces in the label.

4 Press **Enter**.

Note

If you see the message
Bad command or file
name, you typed the
command incorrectly.
Try again.

Check the DOS version

Before

```
C:\>VER
```

Oops!

If you see the message Bad command or file name, you typed the command incorrectly. Try again.

1 **Type VER.**
VER is the version command. You use this command to display the current DOS version.

2 **Press Enter.**
Pressing Enter confirms the command. You see the current DOS version number. The After screen shows the current version as MS-DOS Version 6.20. Your version will be different from the one that appears in the After screen if you use a different DOS version.

After

```
C:\>ver

MS-DOS Version 6.20

C:\>
```

REVIEW

 Type **VER**.

 Press **Enter**.

Check disk space and memory

`C:\>CHKDSK`

1 **Type CHKDSK.**
CHKDSK is the checkdisk command. You use this command to display some basic information about the disk.

2 **Press Enter.**
Pressing Enter confirms the command. DOS checks the disk and displays information in three sections. The first section displays the following information:

> total disk space (in bytes)
>
> number of hidden files (and number of bytes)
>
> number of directories (and number of bytes)
>
> number of user files (and number of bytes)
>
> number of bad sectors if any (in bytes)
>
> number of bytes available on disk

Remember that about 1 million bytes equals one megabyte (M). So if the display shows 1998848, that number would equal about 2M.

The middle section displays information about how space is allocated (assigned). See *Using MS-DOS 6.2,* Special Edition, for information on these lines.

After

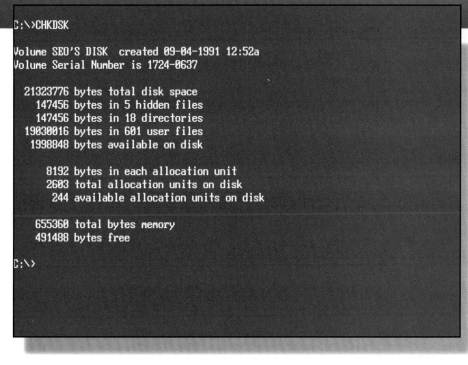

```
C:\>CHKDSK

Volume SEO'S DISK  created 09-04-1991 12:52a
Volume Serial Number is 1724-0637

 21323776 bytes total disk space
   147456 bytes in 5 hidden files
   147456 bytes in 18 directories
 19030016 bytes in 601 user files
  1998848 bytes available on disk

     8192 bytes in each allocation unit
     2603 total allocation units on disk
      244 available allocation units on disk

   655360 total bytes memory
   491488 bytes free

C:\>
```

The last section displays the following information about memory:

    total bytes memory

    total bytes free

Remember that roughly 1 thousand bytes equals one kilobyte (K). So if the display shows 655360, that number would equal about 640K.

REVIEW

 Type **CHKDSK**

 Press **Enter**

Note

The CHKDSK command also lets you repair damage to the data structure. If you see any error messages after using this command, consult *Using MS-DOS 6.2*, Special Edition, for more information.

Set the date

```
C:\>DATE
```

Oops!

To restore the original date, use this same procedure and type the original date when you are prompted.

 1 **Type DATE.**
DATE is the command that you use to set the date.

2 **Press Enter.**
Pressing Enter confirms the command. You see the prompt Current date is, followed by the current date. You also see the prompt Enter new date (mm-dd-yy):.

3 **Type 02-13-93.**
This is the new date you want to enter.

4 **Press Enter.**
Pressing Enter confirms the new date.

After

```
C:\>DATE
Current date is Wed 10-14-1992
Enter new date (mm-dd-yy): 2-13-93

C:\>
```

REVIEW

 Type **DATE**.

 Press **Enter**.

3 Type the new date.

4 Press **Enter**.

> ## Note
>
> Your computer uses the date and time to keep track of when you save files to disk. Be sure that you enter the correct date and time so that your file information is accurate.

> ## Note
>
> Your computer may set the date automatically. If so, this task isn't necessary.

Set the time

```
C:\>TIME
```

1 Type **TIME**.

TIME is the command that you use to set and display the time.

2 Press **Enter**.

Pressing Enter confirms the command. You see the prompt Current time is, followed by the current time. You also see the prompt Enter new time:.

3 Type **14:00:00**.

This is the new time you want to set.

4 Press **Enter**.

Pressing Enter confirms the new time.

After

```
C:\>TIME
Current time is 12:55:10.85a
Enter new time: 14:00:00

C:\>
```

Note

DOS Versions 4, 5, 6, and 6.2 don't require that you enter military time. You can enter 2:00 PM as **2:00p**, for example.

REVIEW

1 Type **TIME**.

2 Press **Enter**.

3 Type the new time.

4 Press **Enter**.

Note

Your computer may automatically set the time. If so, this task may not be necessary.

Set the path

```
C:\>PATH C:\DOS
```

1 **Type PATH.**
PATH is the command that you use to tell DOS which directories it should search to find programs. If a directory is listed in the PATH, you don't have to change to that directory to use a command or start a program.

2 **Press the space bar once.**
Pressing the space bar once inserts a space between the command and the path statement.

3 **Type C:\DOS.**
DOS is the directory that contains all the DOS program files. Your DOS directory might be named differently. If so, type that directory name.

4 **Press Enter.**
Pressing Enter confirms the path.

5 **Type PATH and press Enter.**
This step displays the new path. Notice that if you set the path this way, the new path overrides the path in the AUTOEXEC.BAT file. When you restart the computer, however, the AUTOEXEC.BAT file overrides the path.

After

```
C:\>PATH C:\DOS

C:\>PATH
PATH=C:\DOS

C:\>
```

Note

To include more than one directory in the path, separate the directories by a semi-colon—for example, **C:\DOS;C:\WORD**. Don't include a space between directory names.

REVIEW

 Type **PATH**.

 Press the **space bar once**.

 Type the name of the directory you want to include in the path. Separate each directory name with a semicolon.

4 Press **Enter**.

Note

If you see the message `Directory does not exist`, a nonexistent directory is contained in the path. When you type a command, DOS tries to search in the nonexistent directory.

Check memory information

```
C:\>MEM
```

1 **Type MEM.**
MEM is the command to check memory information.

2 **Press Enter.**
This step executes the command. On-screen you see the total amount of memory your computer has, the amount that is used, and the amount that is free.

Different types of memory are reported: conventional, upper, adapter RAM/ROM, extended, and expanded. This information might come in handy if you are calling for support or if a program requires a certain amount of memory.

After

```
C:\>MEM

Memory Type       Total =  Used  +  Free
----------------  ------  ------  ------
Conventional       640K     94K    546K
Upper              187K     68K    119K
Adapter RAM/ROM    197K    197K      0K
Extended (XMS)    7168K   2440K   4728K
Expanded (EMS)       0K      0K      0K
                  ------  ------  ------
Total memory      8192K   2799K   5393K

Total under 1 MB   827K    162K    665K

Largest executable program size      546K  (559392 bytes)
Largest free upper memory block       92K   (93856 bytes)
MS-DOS is resident in the high memory area.

C:\>
```

REVIEW

1 Type **MEM**.

2 Press **Enter**.

Note

For complete information on all types of memory and their uses, see *Using MS-DOS 6.2*, Special Edition.

Optimize memory

```
C:\>MEMMAKER
```

Oops!

To exit the optimization program, press the F3 key for step 2 or 3 of the Task section.

1 **Type MEMMAKER.**
This command is used to optimize the memory on your system. DOS will check your hardware, make changes to how the system is set up, and restart your computer twice. The optimization is automatic. You don't really need to know what the changes are; you need to know only that the changes should speed up your computer use.

A description of how MEMMAKER works appears on-screen. You then have the option to continue or exit.

2 **Press Enter.**
This step displays the next screen, which tells you the two methods of optimizing memory: Express and Custom. If you are an experienced user, you can use the Custom option. See *Using MS-DOS 6.2, Special Edition,* for complete information. For most purposes, the Express option—the default—will do.

3 **Press Enter.**
This step selects the Express option. DOS checks your hard drive and then displays a message telling you that the computer will be restarted.

4 **Press Enter.**
The computer restarts. DOS checks the memory settings and determines the best settings. A message appears stating that the

After

```
C:\>
```

computer will be restarted again so that the new settings will be in effect.

 Press Enter.
The computer restarts. You see a message that asks whether your system is working properly.

6 **Press Enter.**
This step tells DOS that the startup was okay. You see a message that the optimization is finished. A table shows the changes that were made.

7 **Press Enter.**
This step exits the optimization program. You return to the DOS prompt.

REVIEW

1 Type **MEMMAKER**.

2 Press **Enter**.

3 Press **Enter** each time you are prompted.

Defragment a disk

Select the drive you wish to optimize.

```
     A:
     B:
     C:                OK
                     Cancel
```

Status
Cluster 2   0%

Elapsed Time: 00:00:00
Full Optimization

Legend
- – Used   – Unused
r – Reading   W – Writing
B – Bad   X – Unmovable
Drive ?:   1 block = 0 clusters

Select drive letter and press OK to continue   Microsoft Defrag

To cancel the optimization, select Cancel for step 3. Or press the Esc key and type x for step 4.

1 **Back up your hard disk.**
Be sure to back up your entire hard disk before you run this program. For information, see *TASK: Back up selected directories* and *TASK: Back up selected files*.

2 **Type DEFRAG.**
This command starts the defragmenter program. Before you run this program, you may want to back up your hard drive.

3 **Press Enter.**
This step starts the defragmenter program. You are prompted to select the drive to optimize. By default, drive C is selected. The Before screen shows this step.

4 **Press Enter.**
This step selects drive C. DOS analyzes the hard disk and displays a recommendation. The Optimize button is selected.

(If the drive doesn't need to be optimized, you see a note that says so. Press Enter.)

5 **Press Enter.**
This step executes the Optimize option. You see the progress of the optimization on-screen. DOS reads the disk and optimizes the files and directories. When it is complete, you see a message that reads
Finished condensing.

After

```
C:\>
```

 Press Enter.
This step clears the message and displays a message that reads
`Optimization for Drive C Complete`.

 Press Tab twice.
This step highlights the Exit DEFRAG option.

8 **Press Enter.**
This step selects the Exit DEFRAG option. You return to the DOS prompt.

REVIEW

1 Back up your entire hard drive.

2 Type **DEFRAG**.

3 Press **Enter**.

4 Select the drive you want to optimize and press **Enter**.

5 Press **Enter** twice.

6 Press **Tab** twice to select the Exit DEFRAG option.

7 Press **Enter**.

Note

When DOS saves a file, it sometimes cannot save all the pieces of the file next to each other. Files become fragmented—scattered across the disk. Each time you load a file, DOS has to collect all the respective pieces, and doing so can slow down the computer. Defragmenting the disk puts all the pieces of the files next to each other, which speeds up the computer.

Note

This program is available only with Versions 6 and 6.2 of DOS. DOS 6.2 users can use the DEFRAG command with DBLSPACE—a disk compression program. DOS 6.0 users cannot use the DEFRAG command with DBLSPACE.

Using the
DOS Shell

This section includes the following commands:

- Start the DOS Shell

- Make a menu selection

- Exit the DOS Shell

- Get help

- Display files in another directory

- Expand directories

- Collapse directories

- Expand all directories

- Select a drive

- Display selected files

- Sort files

- Select a file

- Select multiple files

- Select all files

- Copy a file

- Rename a file

- Move a file

- Delete a file

- View file contents

- Search for a file

- Create a directory

- Remove a directory

Start the DOS shell

```
C:\>
```

Oops!

To exit the DOS Shell, see *TASK: Exit the DOS Shell.*

1 **At the DOS prompt, type DOSSHELL.**
DOSSHELL is the command to start the DOS Shell program.

Your computer may be set up to start the DOS Shell automatically. In this case, you don't need to follow this exercise. You will see the DOS Shell screen every time you start your computer.

2 **Press Enter.**

Pressing Enter confirms the command. You see a message as DOS reads the disk information and counts the files and directories. Then you see the DOS Shell screen.

The first line of the screen lists the program name—MS-DOS Shell. Below the title you see the menu bar. The DOS Shell has its own menu system. Menus include File, Options, View, Tree, and Help.

Below the menu bar, you see the name of the current directory—in this case, the root or main directory.

The next part of the screen shows the drive icons. An icon is a pictorial representation of each drive on your computer.

On the left side of the middle of the screen, you see the Directory Tree window. This window contains icons that look like folders. Each folder represents a directory. These are called directory icons.

After

The directories are listed in alphabetical order. Note that some directory icons have a + (plus sign) on them. This symbol indicates that these directories contain other directories. You can expand and collapse the directories shown. (See other tasks in this section for more information.)

The right side of the middle of the screen, called the *file list*, lists the files in the current directory.

The bottom of the screen is called the program list. You use this area to start DOS applications and utilities. See *Using MS-DOS 6.2,* Special Edition, for complete information on using the program list.

REVIEW

1 At the DOS prompt, type **DOSSHELL**.

2 Press **Enter**.

Note

The DOS shell is included only in DOS 5 and 6 (DOS 4 also had a shell, but it worked differently.) A shell is not included with DOS 6.2. If you have DOS 5 or 6 Shell in your DOS directory, the DOS 6.2 upgrade version enables you to continue using it. The shell is available separately on the MS-DOS 6.2 Supplemental Disk.

Note

You can move around four areas of the screen: the drive icon area, the Directory Tree window, the file list, and the program list. Press Tab to move forward from area to area. Press Shift-Tab to move backward.

Note

If Main doesn't appear at the bottom of the screen, press the Alt-V key combination. Then select Program/File Lists. The view might be set to single file list.

Make a menu selection

```
                        MS-DOS Shell
 File  Options  View  Tree  Help
 C:\
 ⊟A   ⊟B   ■C                    ▷

              Directory Tree                      C:\*.*
    C:\                      ↑    ■ AUTOEXEC.BAT      247   06-28-91 ↑
    ├─┤+│ 123R23                    COMMAND .COM   47,867   03-08-91
    ├─┤+│ AFTERDRK                  CONFIG  .SYS      256   06-25-91
    ├─┤+│ AMIPRO                    DEFAULT .BAK    1,797   08-07-91
    ├───  COLLAGE                   FONTWID .BAT       50   07-26-90
    ├─┤+│ DOS                       HIMEM   .SYS   11,304   05-01-90
    ├─┤+│ EXCEL                     IMAGE   .BAK   94,208   09-05-91
    ├───  EZDFIGS                   IMAGE   .DAT   94,208   09-05-91
    ├─┤+│ EZFIGS                    NDOS    .COM   11,845   06-06-91
    ├───  FONTS                     NDOS    .OVL   73,612   06-06-91
    ├─┤+│ HG3                       TREEINFO.NCD    1,883   09-05-91
    ├───  MOUSE1                    VP      .BAT      128   01-29-91
    ├───  NORTON                    WINA20  .386    9,349   03-08-91
    ├───  PCFILE             ↓                                       ↓
                                  Main
    ▭ Command Prompt                                                 ↑
    ▭ Editor
    ▭ MS-DOS QBasic
    ▦ Disk Utilities




                                                                    ↓
 F10=Actions   Shift+F9=Command Prompt                        9:55a
```

Oops!

To close a menu without making a selection, press the Esc key.

---

1 **Press Alt.**

Pressing the Alt key activates the menu bar. The first menu, File, is selected.

2 **Type F.**

Typing F opens the File menu. You see a list of File commands.

To select the menu to open, you can either press the Alt key and type the underlined letter in the menu name, or you can press Alt and use the arrow keys to move to the menu name and then press Enter.

3 **Type x.**

Typing x selects the Exit command. The command is executed. In this case, you return to the DOS prompt. For other commands, you might see a dialog box that prompts you for additional information.

To select a command, you can either type the underlined letter in the command name, or you can use the arrow keys to move to the command name and then press Enter.

After

Note

If a command is dimmed or missing, that command is not available for the current window. If the cursor is in the Directory Tree window, for example, the Copy command is not available because you cannot copy directories.

REVIEW

 1 Press **Alt**.

2 Type the underlined letter of the menu name or use the arrow keys to move to the menu name and then press **Enter**.

3 Type the underlined letter of the command name. You also can use the arrow keys to move to the command name and then press **Enter**.

Note

You can use the mouse to make a menu selection. Just click on the menu name, and then click on the command name.

Exit the DOS shell

```
                          MS-DOS Shell
 File   Options   View   Tree   Help
C:\
[==]A   [==]B   [==]C                    ⌐

        Directory Tree                            C:\*.*
  [□] C:\                        ↑    [=] AUTOEXEC .BAT        247   06-28-91  ↑
     [+] 123R23                       [=] COMMAND  .COM     47,867   03-08-91
     [+] AFTERDRK                     [=] CONFIG   .SYS        256   06-25-91
     [+] AMIPRO                       [=] DEFAULT  .BAK      1,797   08-07-91
     [ ] COLLAGE                      [=] FONTWID  .BAT         50   07-26-90
     [+] DOS                          [=] HIMEM    .SYS     11,304   05-01-90
     [+] EXCEL                        [=] IMAGE    .BAK     94,208   09-05-91
     [ ] EZDFIGS                      [=] IMAGE    .DAT     94,208   09-05-91
     [+] EZFIGS                       [=] NDOS     .COM     11,845   06-06-91
     [ ] FONTS                        [=] NDOS     .OVL     73,612   06-06-91
     [+] HG3                          [=] TREEINFO .NCD      1,883   09-05-91
     [ ] MOUSE1                       [=] VP       .BAT        128   01-29-91
     [ ] NORTON                       [=] WINA20   .386      9,349   03-08-91
     [ ] PCFILE                  ↓                                            ↓
                                         Main
  [=] Command Prompt                                                         ↑
  [=] Editor
  [=] MS-DOS QBasic
  [==] Disk Utilities



                                                                            ↓
 F10=Actions   Shift+F9=Command Prompt                             9:55a
```

Oops!

To restart the DOS
Shell, type DOSSHELL
at the DOS prompt.

1 **Press Alt.**
Pressing the Alt key activates the menu bar. The first menu, File, is
highlighted.

2 **Type F.**
Typing F opens the File menu. You see a list of File commands.

3 **Type x.**
Typing x selects the Exit command. You return to the DOS prompt.

After

C:\>

REVIEW

1 Press **Alt**.

2 Type **F** to open the File menu.

3 Type **x** to select the Exit command.

SHORTCUT

Press the Alt-F4 key com-
bination or the F3 key
to select the File Exit
command.

Get help

```
                         MS-DOS Shell
  File   Options   View   Tree   Help
  C:\
  ⊟A    ⊟B    ▇C          ┌─────────────┐
                          │ Index      ▹│
        Directory Tree    │ Keyboard    │        C:\*.*
  ┌─ C:\                  │ Shell Basics│
  ├─[+] 123R23            │ Commands    │ UTOEXEC.BAT    247   06-28-91 ↑
  ├─[+] AFTERDRK          │ Procedures  │ OMMAND .COM  47,867  03-08-91
  ├─[+] AMIPRO            │ Using Help  │ ONFIG  .SYS     256  06-25-91
  ├─  COLLAGE             │             │ EFAULT .BAK   1,797  08-07-91
  ├─  DOS                 │ About Shell │ ONTWID .BAT      50  07-26-90
  ├─[+] EXCEL             └─────────────┘ IMEM   .SYS  11,304  05-01-90
  ├─  EZDFIGS                      🖺  IMAGE  .BAK  94,208  09-05-91
  ├─  EZFIGS                       🖺  IMAGE  .DAT  94,208  09-05-91
  ├─  FONTS                           NDOS   .COM  11,845  06-06-91
  ├─[+] HG3                        🖺  NDOS   .OVL  73,612  06-06-91
  ├─  MOUSE1                       🖺  TREEINFO.NCD  1,883  09-05-91
  ├─  NORTON                          VP     .BAT     128  01-29-91
  └─  PCFILE              ↓         🖺  WINA20 .386   9,349  03-08-91  ↓
                              Main
  ▭  Command Prompt                                                    ↑
  ▭  Editor
  ▭  MS-DOS QBasic
  ▦  Disk Utilities
                                                                       ↓
  F10=Actions   Shift+F9=Command Prompt                          9:55a
```

Oops!

To close the Help window, press the Esc key.

1 **Start the DOS Shell.**
For help with this step, see *TASK: Start the DOS Shell*. If the DOS Shell is already started, skip this step.

2 **Press Alt.**
Pressing the Alt key activates the menu bar.

3 **Type H.**
Typing H opens the Help menu. You see a list of Help commands.

4 **Type I.**
Typing I selects the Index command. You see an explanation of how to select a topic and an index of topics.

5 **Press Tab until you highlight Movement Keys.**
This step selects the Movement Keys topic. Pressing the Shift-Tab key combination moves the cursor backward through the list. You may not be able to see the selected topic within the window. To scroll through the window, press ↑ or ↓. The selected topic is boxed. (On color monitors, it also appears in a different color.)

6 **Press Enter.**
Pressing Enter displays help about the selected topic—in this case, about movement keys.

After

7 **Press Esc.**
Pressing the Esc key closes the Help window.

REVIEW

1 Start the DOS Shell.

2 Press **Alt** to activate the menu bar.

3 Type **H** to open the Help menu.

4 Type **I** to select the Index command.

5 Press **Tab** until you highlight the command you want.

6 Press **Enter** to display Help.

7 Press **Esc** to close the Help window.

Note

You can use other Help options. For more information, see *Using MS-DOS 6.2*, Special Edition.

Display files in another directory

```
                              MS-DOS Shell
   File   Options   View   Tree   Help
   C:\
   ⊟A    ⊟B    ▬C

                Directory Tree                     C:\*.*
   ┌─ C:\                              ↑  □ AUTOEXEC.BAT      247   06-28-91  ↑
   ├─┬ 123R23                             □ COMMAND .COM   47,867   03-08-91
   ├─┬ AFTERDRK                           ▣ CONFIG  .SYS      256   06-25-91
   ├─┬ AMIPRO                             □ DEFAULT .BAK      797   08-07-91
   ├── COLLAGE                            □ FONTWID .BAT       50   07-26-90
   ├─┬ DOS                                ▣ HIMEM   .SYS   11,304   05-01-90
   ├─┬ EXCEL                              ▣ IMAGE   .BAK   94,208   09-05-91
   ├── EZDFIGS                            ▣ IMAGE   .DAT   94,208   09-05-91
   ├── EZFIGS                             □ NDOS    .COM   11,845   06-06-91
   ├── FONTS                              ▣ NDOS    .OVL   73,612   06-06-91
   ├─┬ HG3                                ▣ TREEINFO.NCD    1,883   09-05-91
   ├── MOUSE1                             ▣ UP      .BAT      128   01-29-91
   ├── NORTON                             ▣ WINA20  .386    9,349   03-08-91
   ├── PCFILE                          ↓                                     ↓
                                  Main
   □ Command Prompt                                                         ↑
   □ Editor
   □ MS-DOS QBasic
   ▤ Disk Utilities



   F10=Actions   Shift+F9=Command Prompt                           9:57a
```

Oops!

Be sure to press Tab to move to the Directory Tree window. Pressing ↓ in the drive icon window does nothing; pressing ↓ in the file list selects a file.

1 **Start the DOS Shell.**
For help with this step, see *TASK: Start the DOS Shell*. If the DOS Shell is already started, skip this step.

2 **Press Tab until the Directory Tree window is highlighted.**
This step moves you to the Directory Tree window.

3 **Press ↓ until the DOS directory is highlighted.**
Pressing ↓ moves you through the list of directories. As a new directory is highlighted, the files in that directory appear in the file list. When you move to the DOS directory, for example, you see in the right window the files in that directory.

After

```
                        MS-DOS Shell
 File  Options  View  Tree  Help
C:\DOS
⊟A    ⊟B    ▬C

        Directory Tree                    C:\DOS\*.*
    ┌─ C:\                      ↑  📄 4201    .CPI      6,404  03-08-91  ↑
       ┌┬ 123R23                   📄 4208    .CPI        720  03-08-91
       ┌┬ AFTERDRK                 📄 5202    .CPI        395  03-08-91
       ┌┬ AMIPRO                   📄 ANSI    .SYS      9,029  03-08-91
       ┌┬ COLLAGE                  📄 APPEND  .EXE     10,774  03-08-91
       ┌┬ DOS                      📄 ASSIGN  .COM      6,399  03-08-91
       ┌┬ EXCEL                    📄 ATTRIB  .EXE     15,796  03-08-91
       ┌┬ EZDFIGS                  📄 BACKUP  .EXE     36,092  03-08-91
       ┌┬ EZFIGS                   📄 CHKDSK  .EXE     16,200  03-08-91
       ┌┬ FONTS                    📄 COMMAND .COM     47,867  03-08-91
       ┌┬ HG3                      📄 COMP    .EXE     14,282  03-08-91
       ┌┬ MOUSE1                   📄 COUNTRY .SYS     16,741  03-08-91
       ┌┬ NORTON                   📄 DEBUG   .EXE     20,634  03-08-91
       ┌┬ PCFILE                ↓  📄 DELOLDOS.EXE     17,660  03-08-91  ↓
                              Main
  ☐ Command Prompt                                                       ↑
  ☐ Editor
  ☐ MS-DOS QBasic
  ▤ Disk Utilities




 F10=Actions   Shift+F9=Command Prompt                          9:57a   ↓
```

REVIEW

1 Start the DOS Shell.

2 Press **Tab** to move to the Directory Tree window.

3 Press ↓ or ↑ to highlight the directory you want.

Note

To see other direc-
tories, expand the
directory listing. See
*TASK: Expand
directories* and *TASK:
Expand all directories.*

Note

To select a directory
by using the mouse,
click on the directory
name.

Expand directories

Oops!

If the command is dimmed, that command is not available for the selected directory. The directory probably does not contain other directories. Be sure that the directory icon has a plus sign on it before you try to expand it.

1 Start the DOS Shell.
For help with this step, see *TASK: Start the DOS Shell*. If the DOS Shell is already started, skip this step.

2 Press Tab until you move to the Directory Tree window.
This step moves you to the Directory Tree window. This window lists the current directories.

3 Press ↓ or ↑ until you highlight a directory with an icon that contains a plus sign (+).
In the example, the directory 123R23 is highlighted. If you don't have this directory, highlight one you do have. Make sure that its icon is marked with a plus sign (+). A plus sign indicates that a directory contains other directories. The Before screen shows this step.

4 Press Alt.
Pressing the Alt key activates the menu bar.

5 Type T.
Typing T opens the Tree menu. You see a list of commands.

6 Type B.
Typing B selects the Expand Branch command. All levels of directories within the selected directory (123R23) appear. If these directories contain other directories, you also see these other directories.

After

```
                         MS-DOS Shell
 File  Options  View  Tree  Help
 C:\123R23
 ⊟A   ⊟B   ▬C                                  ▷

        Directory Tree                    C:\123R23\*.*
 ┌─ C:\                          ↑  🖳 123      .CMP    171,469  04-11-91 ↑
    └─ 123R23                        🖳 123      .CNF        429  05-03-91
        ├─ TUTOR                     🖳 123      .DLD      6,640  10-22-90
        ├─ WYSIWYG                   🖳 123      .DYN     14,439  04-11-91
        └─ WYSYGO                    ▭ 123      .EXE     18,368  05-02-91
     ├─ AFTERDRK                     🖳 123      .HLP    711,067  04-07-91
     ├─ AMIPRO                       🖳 123      .LLD     16,419  04-11-91
     ├─ COLLAGE                      🖳 123      .RI      43,582  04-11-91
     ├─ DOS                          🖳 123      .SET     51,493  05-02-91
     ├─ EXCEL                        🖳 123R23   .ICO        766  12-01-89
     ├─ EZDFIGS                      🖳 123R23   .PIF        545  04-25-91
     ├─ EZFIGS                       🖳 ARROW    .CGM        702  01-10-91
     ├─ FONTS                        🖳 AUDITOR  .ADN      9,832  04-08-91
     ├─ HG3                       ↓  🖳 BLOCK1   .FNT      5,732  10-16-90 ↓
                                  Main
 ▭  Command Prompt                                                        ↑
 ▭  Editor
 ▭  MS-DOS QBasic
 ▭  Disk Utilities




                                                                         ↓
 F10=Actions   Shift+F9=Command Prompt                          9:59a
```

Note that the directory icon is now marked with a minus sign (–).
This sign reminds you that you can collapse the directory if you
want. See *TASK: Collapse directories for more information*.

REVIEW

1 Start the DOS Shell.

2 Press **Tab** to move to the Directory Tree window.

3 Press ↓ or ↑ to highlight the directory you want to expand. Make
sure that the icon contains a plus sign (+).

4 Press **Alt** to activate the menu bar.

5 Type **T** to open the Tree menu.

6 Type **B** to select Expand Branch.

Note

To expand just one
level, use the Expand
One Level command
from the Tree menu.

SHORTCUT

Highlight the directory
and then press *
(asterisk) or + (plus) to
expand the directory.

Collapse directories

```
                          MS-DOS Shell
   File   Options   View   Tree   Help
  C:\123R23
  ▭A   ▭B   ▭C                              ⍩

         Directory Tree                  C:\123R23\*.*
  ┌─ C:\                              ↑  ▣  123     .CMP    171,469  04-11-91 ↑
   └─┐ 123R23                            ▣  123     .CNF        429  05-03-91
       ┌ TUTOR                           ▣  123     .DLD      6,640  10-22-90
       ┌ WYSIWYG                         ▣  123     .DYN     14,439  04-11-91
       └ WYSYGO                          ▢  123     .EXE     18,368  05-02-91
     ┌+┐ AFTERDRK                        ▣  123     .HLP    711,867  04-07-91
     ┌+┐ AMIPRO                          ▣  123     .LLD     16,419  04-11-91
     ┌─┐ COLLAGE                         ▣  123     .RI      43,582  04-11-91
     ┌+┐ DOS                             ▣  123     .SET     51,493  05-02-91
     ┌+┐ EXCEL                           ▣  123R23  .ICO        766  12-01-89
     ┌+┐ EZDFIGS                         ▣  123R23  .PIF        545  04-25-91
     ┌+┐ EZFIGS                          ▣  ARROW   .CGM        702  01-10-91
     ┌+┐ FONTS                           ▣  AUDITOR .ADN      9,832  04-08-91
     ┌+┐ HG3                          ↓  ▣  BLOCK1  .FNT      5,732  10-16-90 ↓
                                       Main
  ▭  Command Prompt                                                          ↑
  ▭  Editor
  ▭  MS-DOS QBasic
  ▦  Disk Utilities



                                                                            ↓
  F10=Actions   Shift+F9=Command Prompt                              9:59a
```

Oops!

To expand a directory, see *TASK: Expand directories.*

1 **Start the DOS Shell.**
For help with this step, see *TASK: Start the DOS Shell*. If the DOS Shell is already started, skip this step.

2 **Press Tab until you move to the Directory Tree window.**
This step moves you to the Directory Tree window. This window lists the current directories.

3 **Press ↓ or ↑ until you highlight a directory with an icon that contains a minus sign (–).**
Remember that you first have to expand a directory before you can collapse it. If the directory contains a plus sign (+), expand it first. (See *TASK: Expand directories*.)

In the example, the directory 123R23 is highlighted. If you don't have this directory, highlight one you do have. Make sure that its icon contains a minus sign. The Before screen shows this step.

4 **Press Alt.**
Pressing the Alt key activates the menu bar.

5 **Type T.**
Typing T opens the Tree menu. You see a list of commands.

After

```
                          MS-DOS Shell
 File  Options  View  Tree  Help
 C:\123R23
 ▭A   ▭B   ▭C                                    ▷

      Directory Tree                    C:\123R23\*.*
 ┌─ C:\                          ↑   ▤ 123     .CMP     171,469  04-11-91 ↑
    ┌─ 123R23                        ▤ 123     .CNF         429  05-03-91
    ┌─ AFTERDRK                      ▤ 123     .DLD       6,640  10-22-90
    ┌─ AMIPRO                        ▤ 123     .DYN      14,439  04-11-91
    ┌─ COLLAGE                       ▭ 123     .EXE      18,368  05-02-91
    ┌─ DOS                           ▤ 123     .HLP     711,067  04-07-91
    ┌─ EXCEL                         ▤ 123     .LLD      16,419  04-11-91
    ┌─ EZDFIGS                       ▤ 123     .RI       43,582  04-11-91
    ┌─ EZFIGS                        ▤ 123     .SET      51,493  05-02-91
    ┌─ FONTS                         ▤ 123R23  .ICO         766  12-01-89
    ┌─ HG3                           ▤ 123R23  .PIF         545  04-25-91
    ┌─ MOUSE1                        ▤ ARROW   .CGM         702  01-10-91
    ┌─ NORTON                        ▤ AUDITOR .ADN       9,832  04-08-91
    ┌─ PCFILE                    ↓   ▤ BLOCK1  .FNT       5,732  10-16-90 ↓
                                 Main
 ▭ Command Prompt                                                        ↑
 ▤ Editor
 ▤ MS-DOS QBasic
 ▥ Disk Utilities



                                                                         ↓
 F10=Actions   Shift+F9=Command Prompt                          9:59a
```

6 **Type C.**

Typing C selects the Collapse Branch command and collapses the directory. Only the parent directory appears (the directory that contains the other directories).

REVIEW

1 Start the DOS Shell.

2 Press **Tab** to move to the Directory Tree window.

3 Press ↓ or ↑ to highlight the directory you want to collapse. Be sure that the directory contains a minus sign (–).

4 Press **Alt** to activate the menu bar.

5 Type **T** to open the Tree menu.

6 Type **C** to select Collapse Branch.

Note

If the root directory is selected and you select Collapse Branch, you see C:\ in the Directory Tree window. Use the Expand One Level command to expand directory list to the original list.

SHORTCUT

Highlight the directory and then press – (minus) to collapse the directory.

Expand all directories

```
                        MS-DOS Shell
 File   Options   View   Tree   Help
C:\
▭A    ▭B    ▭C                              �

         Directory Tree                        C:\*.*
  ┌─ C:\                        ▲  ▭ AUTOEXEC.BAT        247   06-28-91 ▲
  ├─[+] 123R23                     ▭ COMMAND .COM     47,867   03-08-91
  ├─[+] AFTERDRK                   ▭ CONFIG  .SYS        256   06-25-91
  ├─[+] AMIPRO                     ▭ DEFAULT .BAK      1,797   08-07-91
  ├─ COLLAGE                       ▭ FONTWID .BAT         50   07-26-90
  ├─[+] DOS                        ▭ HIMEM   .SYS     11,304   05-01-90
  ├─[+] EXCEL                      ▭ IMAGE   .BAK     94,208   09-05-91
  ├─ EZDFIGS                       ▭ IMAGE   .DAT     94,208   09-05-91
  ├─[+] EZFIGS                     ▭ NDOS    .COM     11,845   06-06-91
  ├─ FONTS                         ▭ NDOS    .OVL     73,612   06-06-91
  ├─[+] HG3                        ▭ TREEINFO.NCD      1,883   09-05-91
  ├─ MOUSE1                        ▭ VP      .BAT        128   01-29-91
  ├─ NORTON                        ▭ WINA20  .386      9,349   03-08-91
  ├─ PCFILE                     ▼                               ▼
                             Main
  ▭ Command Prompt                                              ▲
  ▭ Editor
  ▭ MS-DOS QBasic
  ▭ Disk Utilities




                                                               ▼
 F10=Actions   Shift+F9=Command Prompt                    9:59a
```

Oops!

To collapse all the directories (you will see C:\ on-screen), highlight the root directory, and then press the Alt key, type T, and then type C.

1 **Start the DOS Shell.**
For help with this step, see *TASK: Start the DOS Shell*. If the DOS Shell is already started, skip this step.

2 **Press Tab until you move to the Directory Tree window.**
This step moves you to the Directory Tree window. This window lists the current directories.

3 **Make sure that the root directory is highlighted.**
The root directory should be highlighted when you press Tab. If it is not highlighted, use ↑ or ↓ to select this directory. Remember that the root directory is named \ (backslash). For instance, C:\ indicates that the root directory is on drive C.

4 **Press Alt.**
Pressing the Alt key activates the menu bar.

5 **Type T.**
Typing T opens the Tree menu. You see a list of commands.

6 **Type A.**
Typing A selects the Expand All command. All the directories appear.

You can collapse selected branches of the directory. See *TASK: Collapse directories* for more information.

After

```
                        MS-DOS Shell
 File  Options  View  Tree  Help
 C:\
 [==]A    [==]B    [■■]C                              ⌐

       Directory Tree                          C:\*.*
 ┌─ C:\                            ↑  │ [▭] AUTOEXEC.BAT       247   06-28-91 ↑
 └─┬─ 123R23                          │ [▭] COMMAND  .COM    47,867  03-08-91
   │ ├─ TUTOR                         │ [▭] CONFIG   .SYS       256  06-25-91
   │ ├─ WYSIWYG                       │ [▭] DEFAULT  .BAK     1,797  08-07-91
   │ └─ WYSYGO                        │ [▭] FONTWID  .BAT        50  07-26-90
   ├─ AFTERDRK                        │ [▭] HIMEM    .SYS    11,304  05-01-90
   │ ├─ ADMODULE.SDK                  │ [▭] IMAGE    .BAK    94,208  09-05-91
   │ │ └─ BLANKER                     │ [▭] IMAGE    .DAT    94,208  09-05-91
   │ └─ BITMAPS                       │ [▭] NDOS     .COM    11,845  06-06-91
   ├─ AMIPRO                          │ [▭] NDOS     .OVL    73,612  06-06-91
   │ ├─ DOCS                          │ [▭] TREEINFO.NCD      1,883  09-05-91
   │ ├─ DRAWSYM                       │ [▭] VP       .BAT       128  01-29-91
   │ ├─ MACROS                        │ [▭] WINA20   .386     9,349  03-08-91
   │ └─ STYLES                     ↓  │                                        ↓
                                 Main
 [▭] Command Prompt                                                           ↑
 [▭] Editor
 [▭] MS-DOS QBasic
 [▭] Disk Utilities



 F10=Actions   Shift+F9=Command Prompt                             9:59a     ↓
```

REVIEW

1   Start the DOS Shell.

2   Press **Tab** to move to the Directory Tree window.

3   Make sure that the root directory is highlighted.

4   Press **Alt** to activate the menu bar.

5   Type **T** to open the Tree menu.

6   Type **A** to select Expand All.

Select a drive

Oops!

If you get a warning message, make sure that the disk is inserted and the drive door is closed. Then press Enter to select the option named Try to read this disk again.

1 **Start the DOS Shell.**
For help with this step, see *TASK: Start the DOS Shell*. If the DOS Shell is already started, skip this step.

2 **Insert a disk into floppy drive A.**
Every computer has at least one floppy drive, called drive A. You also might have other floppy drives. Insert a disk into drive A of your computer. Be sure to close the drive door.

3 **Press Tab until you move to the drive icon area.**
This step moves you to the drive icon area. The drive icon area is just beneath the menu bar. The cursor may already be in this area.

4 **Press → or ← until you highlight the drive A icon.**
Pressing → or ← selects drive A. (The current position of the cursor will determine whether you need to press → to move right or ← to move left.) The drive letter is highlighted.

5 **Press Enter.**
Pressing Enter displays the directories on this drive in the Directory Tree window and the files in the file list window.

After

Directory Tree

A:\

A:*.*

XTREEOUT.DOC   3,914   08-26-91
XTREEOUT.DOS   2,816   08-26-91

Main

Command Prompt
Editor
MS-DOS QBasic
Disk Utilities

F10=Actions   Shift+F9=Command Prompt   10:09a

REVIEW

1 Start the DOS Shell.

2 Insert a disk into the drive.

3 Press **Tab** to move to the drive icon area.

4 Press → or ← to highlight the drive.

5 Press **Enter**.

Note

To move back to drive C, press → to highlight drive C; then press Enter.

Note

↑ and ↓ do not work in the drive icon window. You must press → and ←.

Display selected files

```
                        MS-DOS Shell
 File  Options  View  Tree  Help
 C:\DOS
 ▭A  ▭B  ▭C                                    ▷

        Directory Tree                    C:\DOS\*.*
 ┌─ C:\                      ↑    📑 4201    .CPI      6,404  03-08-91  ↑
 ├─📁 123R23                      📑 4208    .CPI        720  03-08-91
 ├─📁 AFTERDRK                    📑 5202    .CPI        395  03-08-91
 ├─📁 AMIPRO                      📑 ANSI    .SYS      9,029  03-08-91
 ├─📁 COLLAGE                     📄 APPEND  .EXE     10,774  03-08-91
 ├─📁 DOS                         📄 ASSIGN  .COM      6,399  03-08-91
 ├─📁 EXCEL                       📄 ATTRIB  .EXE     15,796  03-08-91
 ├─📁 EZDFIGS                     📄 BACKUP  .EXE     36,092  03-08-91
 ├─📁 EZFIGS                      📄 CHKDSK  .EXE     16,200  03-08-91
 ├─📁 FONTS                       📄 COMMAND .COM     47,867  03-08-91
 ├─📁 HG3                         📄 COMP    .EXE     14,282  03-08-91
 ├─📁 MOUSE1                      📑 COUNTRY .SYS     16,741  03-08-91
 ├─📁 NORTON                      📄 DEBUG   .EXE     20,634  03-08-91
 ├─📁 PCFILE                  ↓   📄 DELOLDOS.EXE     17,660  03-08-91  ↓
                                Main
 📄 Command Prompt                                                     ↑
 📄 Editor
 📄 MS-DOS QBasic
 ▦ Disk Utilities



 F10=Actions  Shift+F9=Command Prompt                        10:10a    ↓
```

Oops!

To view all files again, follow this same procedure, but type *.* instead of typing *.SYS.

1 **Start the DOS Shell.**
For help with this step, see *TASK: Start the DOS Shell*. If the DOS Shell is already started, skip this step.

2 **Press Tab until you move to the Directory Tree window.**
This step moves the cursor to the Directory Tree window.

3 **Press ↑ or ↓ until the DOS directory is highlighted.**
Pressing ↑ or ↓ highlights the directory for which you want to display files. (The current position of the cursor will determine whether you need to press ↑ to move up or ↓ to move down.) If you don't have a directory named DOS, highlight one that you do have.

4 **Press Alt.**
Pressing the Alt key activates the menu bar.

5 **Type O.**
Typing O opens the Options menu. You see a list of Options commands.

6 **Type F.**
Typing F selects the File Display Options command. You see the File Display Options dialog box. Within this box is a Name: text box that displays *.*. This specification (called star-dot-star) tells the DOS Shell to display all files.

After

7 Type *.SYS.

This step tells the DOS Shell to display files that have any root name, but that have the SYS extension. (* is a wild card that can represent any characters and any number of characters.)

8 Press Enter.

Pressing Enter confirms the command. You see only the SYS files in the file list window.

REVIEW

1 Start the DOS Shell.

2 Press **Tab** to move to the Directory Tree window.

3 Use ↑ or ↓ to highlight the directory for which you want to display selected files.

4 Press **Alt** to activate the menu bar.

5 Type **O** to open the Options menu.

6 Type **F** to select the File Display Options command.

7 In the Name text box, type the file name you want to display. Use wild cards if you want, and press **Enter**.

Note

A wild card is a character that matches any character or characters. The question mark wild card (?) matches a single character. The asterisk wild card (*) matches all characters.

Note

Use this same procedure to list other files. For example, in the Name: text box, type **S*.*** to list all files that start with S. Type **FO*.COM** to match all files that start with FO and have the extension COM. Type **ASSIGN.COM** to display the file named ASSIGN.COM.

Sort files

```
                          MS-DOS Shell
   File  Options  View  Tree  Help
   C:\DOS
   ⊟A    ⊟B    ■C
  ┌──────── Directory Tree ────────┐┌────────── C:\DOS\*.* ──────────┐
  │ ┌─ C:\                        ↑││ ▣ 4201     .CPI    6,404 03-08-91 ↑│
  │   ├─[+] 123R23                 ││ ▣ 4208     .CPI      720 03-08-91  │
  │   ├─[+] AFTERDRK               ││ ▣ 5202     .CPI      395 03-08-91  │
  │   ├─[+] AMIPRO                 ││ ▣ ANSI     .SYS    9,029 03-08-91  │
  │   ├─[ ] COLLAGE                ││ ▤ APPEND   .EXE   10,774 03-08-91  │
  │   ├─[+] DOS                    ││ ▤ ASSIGN   .COM    6,399 03-08-91  │
  │   ├─[+] EXCEL                  ││ ▤ ATTRIB   .EXE   15,796 03-08-91  │
  │   ├─[+] EZDFIGS                ││ ▤ BACKUP   .EXE   36,092 03-08-91  │
  │   ├─[+] EZFIGS                 ││ ▤ CHKDSK   .EXE   16,200 03-08-91  │
  │   ├─[ ] FONTS                  ││ ▤ COMMAND  .COM   47,867 03-08-91  │
  │   ├─[+] HG3                    ││ ▤ COMP     .EXE   14,282 03-08-91  │
  │   ├─[ ] MOUSE1                 ││ ▣ COUNTRY  .SYS   16,741 03-08-91  │
  │   ├─[ ] NORTON                 ││ ▤ DEBUG    .EXE   20,634 03-08-91  │
  │   └─[ ] PCFILE                ↓││ ▤ DELOLDOS .EXE   17,660 03-08-91 ↓│
  ├─────────────────────────── Main ───────────────────────────┐
  │ ▤  Command Prompt                                          ↑│
  │ ▤  Editor                                                   │
  │ ▤  MS-DOS QBasic                                            │
  │ ▦  Disk Utilities                                           │
  │                                                             │
  │                                                            ↓│
  └─────────────────────────────────────────────────────────────┘
   F10=Actions   Shift+F9=Command Prompt               10:10a
```

Oops!

To sort files by name, follow this same procedure, but select Name rather than Extension.

1 **Start the DOS Shell.**
For help with this step, see *TASK: Start the DOS Shell*.

2 **Press Tab until you move to the Directory Tree window.**
This step moves the cursor to the Directory Tree window.

3 **Press ↑ or ↓ until the DOS directory is highlighted.**
Pressing ↑ or ↓ highlights the directory for which you want to display and sort files.

4 **Press Alt.**
Pressing the Alt key activates the menu bar.

5 **Type O.**
This step opens the Options menu.

6 **Type F.**
This step selects the File Display Options command. You see the File Display Options dialog box. Within this box is a text box that displays *.*. (See *TASK: Display certain files.*) This box also lists Sort by options, which enable you to specify how items are sorted.

7 **Press Tab three times.**
This step moves the cursor to the Sort by options.

8 **Press ↓.**
Pressing ↓ selects the Extension option. You can tell this option is selected because the button next to the sort name is filled in.

After

This option tells the DOS Shell to sort the files in the directory by extension. (The default list is sorted by name.)

9   **Press Enter.**
Pressing Enter confirms the command.

REVIEW

1   Start the DOS Shell.

2   Press **Tab** to move to the Directory Tree window.

3   Use ↑ or ↓ to highlight the directory for which you want to sort files.

4   Press **Alt** to activate the menu bar.

5   Type **O** to open the Options menu.

6   Type **F** to select the File Display Options command.

7   Press **Tab** to move to the Sort by options.

8   Press ↓ until the sort option you want is selected.

9   Press **Enter**.

Note

You also can sort by date, size, and other options. See *Using MS-DOS 6.2*, Special Edition, for complete information on sort options.

Select
a file

```
                        MS-DOS Shell
 File  Options  View  Tree  Help
C:\
 ⊞A   ⊞B   ▭C
━━━━━━━━━━━━━━━━━━━━━━━━━━━━━━━━━━━━━━━━━━━━━━━━━━━━━━━━
        Directory Tree                   C:\*.*
 ┌─ C:\                        ↑   │ AUTOEXEC.BAT     247  06-28-91  ↑
 ├─┬ 123R23                        │ COMMAND .COM  47,867  03-08-91
 ├─┬ AFTERDRK                      │ CONFIG  .SYS     256  06-25-91
 ├─┬ AMIPRO                        │ DEFAULT .BAK   1,797  08-07-91
 ├─  COLLAGE                       │ FONTWID .BAT      50  07-26-90
 ├─┬ DOS            ⊾              │ HIMEM   .SYS  11,304  05-01-90
 ├─┬ EXCEL                         │ IMAGE   .BAK  94,208  09-05-91
 ├─  EZDFIGS                       │ IMAGE   .DAT  94,208  09-05-91
 ├─┬ EZFIGS                        │ NDOS    .COM  11,845  06-06-91
 ├─  FONTS                         │ NDOS    .OVL  73,612  06-06-91
 ├─┬ HG3                           │ TREEINFO.NCD   1,883  09-05-91
 ├─  MOUSE1                        │ VP      .BAT     128  01-29-91
 ├─  NORTON                        │ WINA20  .386   9,349  03-08-91
 ├─  PCFILE                    ↓   │                                ↓
━━━━━━━━━━━━━━━━━━━━━━━━ Main ━━━━━━━━━━━━━━━━━━━━━━━━
 ▭ Command Prompt                                                   ↑
 ▭ Editor
 ▭ MS-DOS QBasic
 ▭ Disk Utilities



                                                                    ↓
 F10=Actions   Shift+F9=Command Prompt                     10:12a
```

Oops!

If you highlight the wrong file, press ↑ or ↓ to move to the correct file.

1 Start the DOS Shell.

For help with this step, see *TASK: Start the DOS Shell*. If the DOS Shell is already started, skip this step.

2 Press Tab until you move to the Directory Tree window.

This step moves the cursor to the Directory Tree window. The root directory will probably be selected. If it isn't, press ↑ to highlight the root directory.

3 Press Tab to move to the file list.

This step moves the cursor to the file list. You can tell that the file list is selected because the title bar changes color or intensity.

To select a file, you must be in the file list window. If you are in the Directory Tree window, you can press ↓ or ↑ to move among the directories.

4 Press ↑ or ↓ to highlight the file CONFIG.SYS.

This step highlights the file you want to select. If you don't have this file, highlight one you do have. After you select a file, you can perform operations, such as copying it, moving it, deleting it, and so on. See the other tasks in this section.

Note

To select a file by using the mouse, click on the file name.

REVIEW

1 Start the DOS Shell.

2 If necessary, press **Tab** to move to the Directory Tree window; then select the directory that contains the file.

3 Press **Tab** to move to the file list window.

4 Use ↑ or ↓ to highlight the file.

Note

To select a file in another directory, first highlight the directory in the Directory Tree window. The files for the highlighted directory will appear in the file list window. Press Tab to move to the file list window; then select the file.

Select multiple files

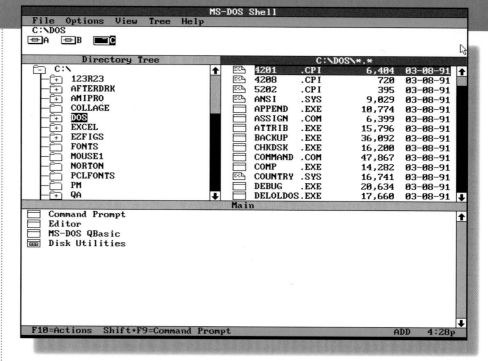

```
                        MS-DOS Shell
 File  Options  View  Tree  Help
 C:\DOS
 ⊟A   ⊟B   ▅▅C
                                                              ⌖
          Directory Tree                     C:\DOS\*.*
 ┌─ C:\                          ↑    ▦ 4201    .CPI      6,404  03-08-91 ↑
    ├─ 123R23                         ▦ 4208    .CPI        720  03-08-91
    ├─ AFTERDRK                       ▦ 5202    .CPI        395  03-08-91
    ├─ AMIPRO                         ▦ ANSI    .SYS      9,029  03-08-91
    ├─ COLLAGE                          APPEND  .EXE     10,774  03-08-91
    ├─ DOS                              ASSIGN  .COM      6,399  03-08-91
    ├─ EXCEL                            ATTRIB  .EXE     15,796  03-08-91
    ├─ EZFIGS                           BACKUP  .EXE     36,092  03-08-91
    ├─ FONTS                            CHKDSK  .EXE     16,200  03-08-91
    ├─ MOUSE1                           COMMAND .COM     47,867  03-08-91
    ├─ NORTON                           COMP    .EXE     14,282  03-08-91
    ├─ PCLFONTS                       ▦ COUNTRY .SYS     16,741  03-08-91
    ├─ PM                               DEBUG   .EXE     20,634  03-08-91
    ├─ QA                        ↓      DELOLDOS.EXE     17,660  03-08-91 ↓
                                  Main
    Command Prompt                                                        ↑
    Editor
    MS-DOS QBasic
 ▦  Disk Utilities



 F10=Actions   Shift+F9=Command Prompt                        ADD    4:28p
```

Oops!

To deselect a file, move the cursor to the file that you want to deselect, and press the space bar again.

1 **Start the DOS Shell.**
For help with this step, see *TASK: Start the DOS Shell*. If the DOS Shell is already started, skip this step.

2 **Press Tab to move to the Directory Tree window.**
This step moves the cursor to the Directory Tree window so that you can select the directory you want.

3 **Press ↑ or ↓ until you highlight the DOS directory.**
This step selects the directory. If you don't have a directory named DOS, select one that you do have.

4 **Press Tab to move to the file list window.**
This step moves the cursor to the file list window so that you can select the files.

5 **Press ↑ or ↓ to move to the file ANSI.SYS.**
This step moves the cursor to the file you want to select. If you don't have a file named ANSI.SYS, select one you do have.

6 **Press Shift-F8.**
This step turns on Add mode. While in Add mode, you can add Selected files.

7 **Press ↓ or ↑ to move to the file ATTRIB.EXE.**
This step moves the cursor to the next file you want to select.

After

```
                          MS-DOS Shell
 File  Options  View  Tree  Help
 C:\DOS
 ▭A    ▭B    ■C                                          ↕

        Directory Tree                         C:\DOS\*.*
  ┌ C:\                              ↑   📄 4201    .CPI      6,404   03-08-91  ↑
  ├─📁 123R23                            📄 4208    .CPI        720   03-08-91
  ├─📁 AFTERDRK                          📄 5202    .CPI        395   03-08-91
  ├─📁 AMIPRO                            📄 ANSI    .SYS      9,029   03-08-91
  ├─📁 COLLAGE                           📄 APPEND  .EXE     10,774   03-08-91
  ├─📁 DOS                               📄 ASSIGN  .COM      6,399   03-08-91
  ├─📁 EXCEL                             📄 ATTRIB  .EXE     15,796   03-08-91
  ├─📁 EZFIGS                            📄 BACKUP  .EXE     36,092   03-08-91
  ├─📁 FONTS                             📄 CHKDSK  .EXE     16,200   03-08-91
  ├─📁 MOUSE1                            📄 COMMAND .COM     47,867   03-08-91
  ├─📁 NORTON                            📄 COMP    .EXE     14,282   03-08-91
  ├─📁 PCLFONTS                          📄 COUNTRY .SYS     16,741   03-08-91
  ├─📁 PM                                📄 DEBUG   .EXE     20,634   03-08-91
  └─📁 QA                            ↓   📄 DELOLDOS.EXE     17,660   03-08-91  ↓
                                   Main
  📄 Command Prompt                                                            ↑
  📄 Editor
  📄 MS-DOS QBasic
  📰 Disk Utilities




 F10=Actions   Shift+F9=Command Prompt                          ADD    4:28p   ↓
```

8   **Press Ctrl-space bar.**
This step selects the ATTRIB.EXE file; both files are selected.

REVIEW

1   Start the DOS Shell.

2   If necessary, press **Tab** to move to the Directory Tree window; then select the directory that contains the files you want to select.

3   Press **Tab** to move to the file list window.

4   Press ↑ or ↓ to move to the file you want to select.

5   Press **Shift-F8**.

6   Continue moving to files and pressing **Ctrl-space bar** until you select all the files you want.

Note

To select a continuous list of files, move the cursor to the first file you want to select. Then hold down the Shift key and use the arrow keys to highlight the other files. Release the Shift key when you have selected the files.

Note

To turn off Add mode, press Shift-F8 again.

Select all files

```
                          MS-DOS Shell
   File  Options  View  Tree  Help
  C:\DOS
  ▭A    ▭B    ▬C

         Directory Tree                     C:\DOS\*.*
  📂 C:\                          ↑  📠 4201    .CPI      6,404  03-08-91  ↑
     ├─📂 123R23                      📰 4208    .CPI        720  03-08-91
     ├─📂 AFTERDRK                    📰 5202    .CPI        395  03-08-91
     ├─📂 AMIPRO                      📰 ANSI    .SYS      9,029  03-08-91
     ├─📂 COLLAGE                     📄 APPEND  .EXE     10,774  03-08-91
     ├─📂 DOS                  ⌖      📄 ASSIGN  .COM      6,399  03-08-91
     ├─📂 EXCEL                       📄 ATTRIB  .EXE     15,796  03-08-91
     ├─📂 EZDFIGS                     📄 BACKUP  .EXE     36,092  03-08-91
     ├─📂 EZFIGS                      📄 CHKDSK  .EXE     16,200  03-08-91
     ├─📂 FONTS                       📄 COMMAND .COM     47,867  03-08-91
     ├─📂 HG3                         📄 COMP    .EXE     14,282  03-08-91
     ├─📂 MOUSE1                      📰 COUNTRY .SYS     16,741  03-08-91
     ├─📂 NORTON                      📄 DEBUG   .EXE     20,634  03-08-91
     └─📂 PCFILE                  ↓   📄 DELOLDOS.EXE     17,660  03-08-91  ↓
                                    Main
  📄 Command Prompt                                                        ↑
  📄 Editor
  📄 MS-DOS QBasic
  🖾 Disk Utilities



  F10=Actions   Shift+F9=Command Prompt                          10:13a  ↓
```

Oops!

To deselect files, press Alt, type F, and then type l (lowercase L) to select the Deselect All command.

1 **Start the DOS Shell.**
For help with this step, see *TASK: Start the DOS Shell*. If the DOS Shell is already started, skip this step.

2 **Press Tab to move to the Directory Tree window.**
This step moves the cursor to the Directory Tree window so that you can first select the directory you want.

3 **Press ↑ or ↓ until you highlight the DOS directory.**
This step selects the directory. If you don't have a directory named DOS, select one that you do have.

4 **Press Tab to move to the file list window.**
This step moves the cursor to the file list window so that you can select the files.

5 **Press Alt.**
Pressing the Alt key activates the menu bar.

6 **Type F.**
This step opens the File menu. You see a list of File commands.

7 **Type S.**
This step chooses the Select All command. All files in the file list are selected.

After

After you highlight the files, you can perform operations on all the selected files. See the other tasks in this section.

REVIEW

1 Start the DOS Shell.

2 If necessary, press **Tab** to move to the Directory Tree window; then select the directory that contains the files you want to select.

3 Press **Tab** to move to the file list window.

4 Press **Alt** to activate the menu bar.

5 Type **F** to open the File menu.

6 Type **S** to select the Select All command.

Note

If the Select All command is dimmed, the command is not available. You probably are not in the file list window. Press the Esc key to close the menu, press Tab to move to the file list window, and then try the command again.

Copy a file

```
                        MS-DOS Shell
 File   Options   View   Tree   Help
 C:\
 ⊟A    ⊟B    ■C
┌─────────Directory Tree─────────┐┌──────────C:\*.*──────────┐
│ ⊟  C:                        ↑ ││ ▣ AUTOEXEC.BAT    247  06-28-91 ↑│
│   ├─┬ 123R23          ▷       ││ ▤ COMMAND .COM  47,867  03-08-91 │
│   ├─┬ AFTERDRK                ││ ▤ CONFIG  .SYS     256  06-25-91 │
│   ├─┬ AMIPRO                  ││ ▤ DEFAULT .BAK   1,797  08-07-91 │
│   ├─┬ COLLAGE                 ││ ▣ FONTWID .BAT      50  07-26-90 │
│   ├─┬ DOS                     ││ ▤ HIMEM   .SYS  11,304  05-01-90 │
│   ├─┬ EXCEL                   ││ ▤ IMAGE   .BAK  94,208  09-05-91 │
│   ├─┬ EZDFIGS                 ││ ▤ IMAGE   .DAT  94,208  09-05-91 │
│   ├─┬ EZFIGS                  ││ ▣ NDOS    .COM  11,845  06-06-91 │
│   ├─┬ FONTS                   ││ ▤ NDOS    .OVL  73,612  06-06-91 │
│   ├─┬ HG3                     ││ ▤ TREEINFO.NCD   1,883  09-05-91 │
│   ├─┬ MOUSE1                  ││ ▣ VP      .BAT     128  01-29-91 │
│   ├─┬ NORTON                  ││ ▤ WINA20  .386   9,349  03-08-91 │
│   ├─┬ PCFILE                ↓ ││                               ↓│
└────────────────────────────────┘└──────────Main───────────┘
┌─────────────────────────────────────────────────────────────┐
│ ▤ Command Prompt                                            ↑│
│ ▤ Editor                                                     │
│ ▤ MS-DOS QBasic                                              │
│ ▦ Disk Utilities                                             │
│                                                              ↓│
└─────────────────────────────────────────────────────────────┘
 F10=Actions   Shift+F9=Command Prompt                   10:14a
```

Oops!

If you change your mind, press the Esc key in the File Copy dialog box.

1 **Start the DOS Shell.**
For help with this step, see *TASK: Start the DOS Shell*.

2 **Press Tab until you move to the Directory Tree window.**
This step moves the cursor to the Directory Tree window. The root directory will probably be selected. If it isn't, press ↑ to highlight the root directory.

3 **Press Tab to move to the file list window.**
You now can select the file you want to copy.

4 **Press ↑ or ↓ until you highlight the file AUTOEXEC.BAT.**
AUTOEXEC.BAT is the file that you want to copy. (The Before screen shows this step.)

5 **Press Alt.**
Pressing the Alt key activates the menu bar.

6 **Type F.**
This step opens the File menu.

7 **Type C.**
This step selects the Copy command. On-screen you see the Copy File dialog box. Inside this dialog box you see two text boxes. The cursor is located in the To: box. You type the name of the copy in this box.

After

```
                          MS-DOS Shell
  File  Options  View  Tree  Help
  C:\
  ⊟A    ⊟B    ▬C
┌──────── Directory Tree ────────┬──────────── C:\*.* ────────────┐
│  ┌─ C:\                      ↑ │  ▭ AUTOEXEC.BAT      247 06-28-91 ↑│
│  ├─┬ 123R23                    │  ▭ AUTOEXEC.OLD   ▷ 247 06-28-91  │
│  ├─┬ AFTERDRK                  │  ▭ COMMAND .COM  47,867 03-08-91  │
│  ├─┬ AMIPRO                    │  ▭ CONFIG  .SYS     256 06-25-91  │
│  ├─┬ COLLAGE                   │  ▭ DEFAULT .BAK   1,797 08-07-91  │
│  ├─┬ DOS                       │  ▭ FONTWID .BAT      50 07-26-90  │
│  ├─┬ EXCEL                     │  ▭ HIMEM   .SYS  11,304 05-01-90  │
│  ├─┬ EZDFIGS                   │  ▭ IMAGE   .BAK  94,208 09-05-91  │
│  ├─┬ EZFIGS                    │  ▭ IMAGE   .DAT  94,208 09-05-91  │
│  ├─┬ FONTS                     │  ▭ NDOS    .COM  11,845 06-06-91  │
│  ├─┬ HG3                       │  ▭ NDOS    .OVL  73,612 06-06-91  │
│  ├─┬ MOUSE1                    │  ▭ TREEINFO.NCD   1,883 09-05-91  │
│  ├─┬ NORTON                    │  ▭ VP      .BAT     128 01-29-91  │
│  └─┬ PCFILE                  ↓ │  ▭ WINA20  .386   9,349 03-08-91 ↓│
├──────────────────────── Main ──────────────────────────────────┤
│  ▭ Command Prompt                                              ↑│
│  ▭ Editor                                                      │
│  ▭ MS-DOS QBasic                                               │
│  ▭ Disk Utilities                                             ↓│
│                                                                │
├────────────────────────────────────────────────────────────────┤
│ F10=Actions  Shift+F9=Command Prompt                    10:14a  │
└────────────────────────────────────────────────────────────────┘
```

 8 Type **AUTOEXEC.OLD.**
AUTOEXEC.OLD is the name of the file you want to create. You will have two copies of the same file: AUTOEXEC.BAT and AUTOEXEC.OLD.

9 Press **Enter.**
Pressing Enter confirms the command. The DOS Shell makes a copy of the file. In the directory listing you see the new file.

REVIEW

 1 Start the DOS Shell.

2 If necessary, press **Tab** to move to the Directory Tree window; then select the directory that contains the file you want to copy.

3 Press **Tab** to move to the file list window.

4 Use ↑ and ↓ to highlight the file you want to copy.

5 Press **Alt** to activate the menu bar.

6 Type **F** to open the File menu.

7 Type **C** to select the Copy command.

8 Type the name of the new file and press **Enter**.

SHORTCUT

You also can press the F8 key to select the File Copy command.

Note

When you edit your AUTOEXEC.BAT file, make a copy of the current file. If the new file doesn't work as expected, you can use the copy to return to the original settings.

Copy a File   **181**

Rename
a file

```
                      MS-DOS Shell
 File  Options  View  Tree  Help
 C:\
 ⊞A  ⊞B  ▄C
┌──────Directory Tree──────┐┌─────────C:\*.*─────────┐
│ ⊟ ░C░                   ↑││ ☐ AUTOEXEC.BAT    247  06-28-91 ↑│
│   ⊞ 123R23             ││ ▣ AUTOEXEC.OLD    247  06-28-91 │
│   ⊞ AFTERDRK           ││ ☐ COMMAND .COM 47,867  03-08-91 │
│   ⊞ AMIPRO             ││ ▣ CONFIG  .SYS    256  06-25-91 │
│   ⊟ COLLAGE            ││ ▣ DEFAULT .BAK  1,797  08-07-91 │
│   ⊞ DOS                ││ ☐ FONTWID .BAT     50  07-26-90 │
│   ⊞ EXCEL              ││ ▣ HIMEM   .SYS 11,304  05-01-90 │
│   ⊟ EZDFIGS            ││ ▣ IMAGE   .BAK 94,208  09-05-91 │
│   ⊞ EZFIGS             ││ ▣ IMAGE   .DAT 94,208  09-05-91 │
│   ⊟ FONTS              ││ ▣ NDOS    .COM 11,845  06-06-91 │
│   ⊞ HG3                ││ ▣ NDOS    .OVL 73,612  06-06-91 │
│   ⊟ MOUSE1             ││ ▣ TREEINFO.NCD  1,883  09-05-91 │
│   ⊟ NORTON             ││ ▣ VP      .BAT    128  01-29-91 │
│   ⊟ PCFILE            ↓││ ▣ WINA20  .386  9,349  03-08-91 ↓│
└──────────────────────────┘└───────Main───────────────────┘
 ☐ Command Prompt                                          ↑
 ☐ Editor
 ☐ MS-DOS QBasic
 ▦ Disk Utilities


                                                           ↓
 F10=Actions   Shift+F9=Command Prompt              10:14a
```

Oops!

Follow this same procedure to return the file to its original name.

1 **Start the DOS Shell.**
For help with this step, see *TASK: Start the DOS Shell*.

2 **Press Tab until you move to the Directory Tree window.**
This step moves the cursor to the Directory Tree window. The root directory will probably be selected. If it isn't, press ↑ to highlight the root directory.

3 **Press Tab to move to the file list window.**
You now can select the file you want to rename.

4 **Press ↓ until you highlight the file AUTOEXEC.OLD.**
AUTOEXEC.OLD is the file that you want to rename. (The Before screen shows this step.)

5 **Press Alt.**
Pressing the Alt key activates the menu bar.

6 **Type F.**
This step opens the File menu.

7 **Type n.**
This step selects the Rename command. On-screen you see the Rename File dialog box. Inside this dialog box you see two text boxes. You type the new name in the New name: text box.

After

8 **Type AUTOEXEC.BAK.**
AUTOEXEC.BAK is the new file name you want to assign.

9 **Press Enter.**
Pressing Enter confirms the command. The DOS Shell renames a copy of the file. In the directory listing, you see the file listed with the new name.

REVIEW

1 Start the DOS Shell.

2 If necessary, press **Tab** to move to the Directory Tree window; then select the directory that contains the file you want to rename.

3 Press **Tab** to move to the file list window.

4 Use ↑ or ↓ to highlight the file you want to rename.

5 Press **Alt** to activate the menu bar.

6 Type **F** to open the File menu.

7 Type **n** to select the Rename command.

8 Type the name of the new file and press **Enter.**

Note

If you change your mind and don't want to rename the file, press the Esc key in the File Rename dialog box.

Note

If you type a name that already exists, you see an alert box that tells you access is denied. Type 2 and press Enter to return to the dialog box; then try again.

Move
a file

```
                          MS-DOS Shell
 File  Options  View  Tree  Help
 C:\
 ⊟A    ⊟B   ■C
              Directory Tree                           C:\*.*
        C:\                              ↑  ▤ AUTOEXEC.BAK        247   06-28-91 ↑
     ⊞  123R23                              □ AUTOEXEC.BAT        247   06-28-91
     ⊞  AFTERDRK                            □ COMMAND .COM     47,867   03-08-91
     ⊞  AMIPRO                              ▤ CONFIG  .SYS        256   06-25-91
        COLLAGE                             □ DEFAULT .BAK      1,797   08-07-91
     ⊞  DOS                                 □ FONTWID .BAT         50   07-26-90
     ⊞  EXCEL                               ▤ HIMEM   .SYS     11,304   05-01-90
        EZDFIGS                             ▤ IMAGE   .BAK     94,208   09-05-91
     ⊞  EZFIGS                              ▤ IMAGE   .DAT     94,208   09-05-91
        FONTS                               ▤ NDOS    .COM     11,845   06-06-91
     ⊞  HG3                                 ▤ NDOS    .OVL     73,612   06-06-91
        MOUSE1                              ▤ TREEINFO.NCD      1,883   09-05-91
        NORTON                              ▤ VP      .BAT        128   01-29-91
        PCFILE                           ↓  ▤ WINA20  .386      9,349   03-08-91 ↓
                                          Main
        Command Prompt                                                           ↑
        Editor
        MS-DOS QBasic
     ▦  Disk Utilities



 F10=Actions  Shift+F9=Command Prompt                              10:14a
```

Oops!

If you change your mind and don't want to move the file, press the Esc key in the File Move dialog box.

1 **Start the DOS Shell.**
For help with this step, see *TASK: Start the DOS Shell*.

2 **Press Tab until you move to the Directory Tree window.**
This step moves the cursor to the Directory Tree window. The root directory will probably be selected. If it isn't, press ↑ to highlight the root directory.

3 **Press Tab to move to the file list window.**
You now can select the file you want to move.

4 **Press ↑ or ↓ until you highlight the file AUTOEXEC.BAK.**
AUTOEXEC.BAK is the file that you want to move. (The Before screen shows this step.)

5 **Press Alt.**
Pressing the Alt key activates the menu bar.

6 **Type F.**
This step opens the File menu.

7 **Type M.**
This step selects the Move command. On-screen you see the Move File dialog box. Inside this dialog box you see two text boxes. You type the new location in the To: box.

After

8 Type **C:\DOS.**

C:\DOS is the location where you want to move the file. With this command, you are moving the file to the DOS directory.

9 **Press Enter.**

Pressing Enter confirms the command. The DOS Shell moves the file. The file entry is moved to the new directory and no longer appears in the current directory listing.

REVIEW

1 Start the DOS Shell.

2 If necessary, press **Tab** to move to the Directory Tree window; then select the directory that contains the file you want to move.

3 Press **Tab** to move to the file list window.

4 Use ↑ or ↓ to highlight the file you want to move.

5 Press **Alt** to activate the menu bar.

6 Type **F** to open the File menu.

7 Type **M** to select the Move command.

8 Type the location for the file and press **Enter.**

Note

Don't move a file that needs to be in a specific directory. For example, don't move any program files (files with the extension COM, EXE, or BAT).

SHORTCUT

Press F7 to select the File Move command.

Move a File **185**

Delete a file

```
                        MS-DOS Shell
 File  Options  View  Tree  Help
 C:\DOS
 ⊟A  ⊟B  ■C
        Directory Tree                    C:\DOS\*.*
  ┌─ C:\                          ↑   ▤ 4201     .CPI      6,404   03-08-91 ↑
  ├─┤ 123R23                          ▤ 4208     .CPI        720   03-08-91
  ├─┤ AFTERDRK                        ▤ 5202     .CPI        395   03-08-91
  ├─┤ AMIPRO                          ▤ ANSI     .SYS      9,029   03-08-91
  ├─ COLLAGE                          ▢ APPEND   .EXE     10,774   03-08-91
  ├─┤ DOS                             ▢ ASSIGN   .COM      6,399   03-08-91
  ├─┤ EXCEL                           ▢ ATTRIB   .EXE     15,796   03-08-91
  ├─ EZDFIGS                          ▤ AUTOEXEC .BAK        247   06-28-91
  ├─ EZFIGS                           ▢ BACKUP   .EXE     36,092   03-08-91
  ├─ FONTS                            ▢ CHKDSK   .EXE     16,200   03-08-91
  ├─┤ HG3                             ▢ COMMAND  .COM     47,867   03-08-91
  ├─ MOUSE1                           ▢ COMP     .EXE     14,282   03-08-91
  ├─ NORTON                           ▤ COUNTRY  .SYS     16,741   03-08-91
  ├─ PCFILE                       ↓   ▢ DEBUG    .EXE     20,634   03-08-91 ↓
                                  Main
  ▢ Command Prompt                                                          ↑
  ▤ Editor
  ▤ MS-DOS QBasic
  ⊞ Disk Utilities




                                                                           ↓
 F10=Actions   Shift+F9=Command Prompt                           10:16a
```

Oops!

If you change your mind and don't want to delete a file, press the Esc key (instead of Enter) in the Delete File Confirmation box.

1 **Start the DOS Shell.**
For help with this step, see *TASK: Start the DOS Shell*. If the DOS Shell is already started, skip this step.

2 **Press Tab to move to the Directory Tree window.**
This step moves the cursor to the Directory Tree window so that you can select the directory.

3 **Press ↑ or ↓ until you highlight the DOS directory.**
This step selects the DOS directory. If you don't have a directory named DOS, select one that you do have.

4 **Press Tab to move to the file list window.**
This step moves the cursor to the file list window so that you can select the file you want to delete.

5 **Press ↑ or ↓ until you highlight the file AUTOEXEC.BAK.**
AUTOEXEC.BAK is the file that you want to delete. If you don't have this file, select one you do have. (The Before screen shows this step.) Be sure to select a file that you don't need.

6 **Press Alt.**
Pressing the Alt key activates the menu bar.

7 **Type F.**
This step opens the File menu.

After

```
                              MS-DOS Shell
  File  Options  View  Tree  Help
  C:\DOS
  [=]A   [=]B   [==]C

  ┌──────────Directory Tree──────────┐┌───────────C:\DOS\*.*───────────┐
  │ ┌─ C:\                        ↑  ││  4201    .CPI       6,404  03-08-91 ↑│
  │  ├─┤+│ 123R23                 │  ││  4208    .CPI         720  03-08-91 │
  │  ├─┤+│ AFTERDRK               │  ││  5202    .CPI         395  03-08-91 │
  │  ├─┤+│ AMIPRO                 │  ││  ANSI    .SYS       9,029  03-08-91 │
  │  ├─┤ │ COLLAGE                │  ││  APPEND  .EXE      10,774  03-08-91 │
  │  ├─┤ │ DOS                    │  ││  ASSIGN  .COM       6,399  03-08-91 │
  │  ├─┤+│ EXCEL                  │  ││  ATTRIB  .EXE      15,796  03-08-91 │
  │  ├─┤ │ EZDFIGS                │  ││  BACKUP  .EXE      36,092  03-08-91 │
  │  ├─┤+│ EZFIGS                 │  ││  CHKDSK  .EXE      16,200  03-08-91 │
  │  ├─┤ │ FONTS                  │  ││  COMMAND .COM      47,867  03-08-91 │
  │  ├─┤+│ HG3                    │  ││  COMP    .EXE      14,282  03-08-91 │
  │  ├─┤ │ MOUSE1                 │  ││  COUNTRY .SYS      16,741  03-08-91 │
  │  ├─┤ │ NORTON                 │  ││  DEBUG   .EXE      20,634  03-08-91 │
  │  └─┤ │ PCFILE                 ↓  ││  DELOLDOS.EXE      17,660  03-08-91 ↓│
  ┌────────────────────────────Main────────────────────────────────┐
  │ ┌─┐ Command Prompt                                           ↑  │
  │ ┌─┐ Editor                                                      │
  │ ┌─┐ MS-DOS QBasic                                               │
  │ ┌─┐ Disk Utilities                                             │
  │                                                                 │
  │                                                             ↓   │
  └─────────────────────────────────────────────────────────────────┘
  F10=Actions  Shift+F9=Command Prompt                       10:16a
```

 8 **Type D.**
This step selects the Delete command. On-screen you see the Delete File Confirmation alert box.

 9 **Press Enter.**
Pressing Enter confirms the deletion and deletes the file. The file no longer appears in the current directory listing.

REVIEW

 1 Start the DOS Shell.

2 If necessary, press **Tab** to move to the Directory Tree window; then select the directory that contains the file you want to delete.

3 Press **Tab** to move to the file list window.

4 Use ↑ or ↓ to highlight the file you want to delete.

5 Press **Alt** to activate the menu bar.

6 Type **F** to open the File menu.

7 Type **D** to select the Delete command.

 8 Press **Enter** to confirm the deletion.

Note

Be sure that you don't delete a file you need. Double-check before you confirm the deletion.

SHORTCUT

You also can press the Del key to select the File Delete command.

Delete a File **187**

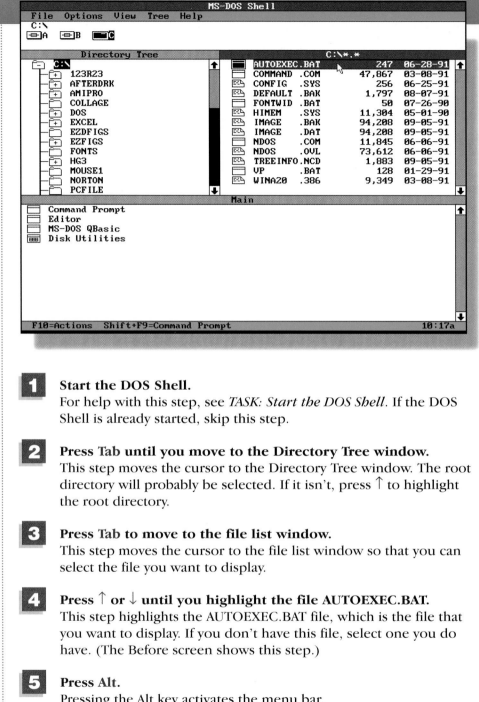

View file contents

1 Start the DOS Shell.
For help with this step, see *TASK: Start the DOS Shell*. If the DOS Shell is already started, skip this step.

2 Press Tab until you move to the Directory Tree window.
This step moves the cursor to the Directory Tree window. The root directory will probably be selected. If it isn't, press ↑ to highlight the root directory.

3 Press Tab to move to the file list window.
This step moves the cursor to the file list window so that you can select the file you want to display.

4 Press ↑ or ↓ until you highlight the file AUTOEXEC.BAT.
This step highlights the AUTOEXEC.BAT file, which is the file that you want to display. If you don't have this file, select one you do have. (The Before screen shows this step.)

5 Press Alt.
Pressing the Alt key activates the menu bar.

6 Type F.
Typing F opens the File menu.

7 Type V.
Typing V selects the View File Contents command. On-screen you see the file contents. (What you see may differ from the After screen because your AUTOEXEC.BAT file may contain other commands.)

After

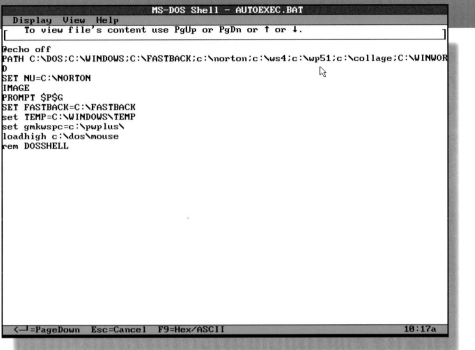

```
                    MS-DOS Shell - AUTOEXEC.BAT
 Display  View  Help
     To view file's content use PgUp or PgDn or ↑ or ↓.

@echo off
PATH C:\DOS;C:\WINDOWS;C:\FASTBACK;c:\norton;c:\ws4;c:\wp51;c:\collage;C:\WINWOR
D
SET NU=C:\NORTON
IMAGE
PROMPT $P$G
SET FASTBACK=C:\FASTBACK
set TEMP=C:\WINDOWS\TEMP
set gmkwspc=c:\pwplus\
loadhigh c:\dos\mouse
rem DOSSHELL




 ←┘=PageDown  Esc=Cancel  F9=Hex/ASCII                          10:17a
```

Note

Some files (especially program files) contain characters that DOS cannot display. You may see strange characters or many numbers on-screen if you display this type of file. Press the Esc key to stop the display.

8 **Press Esc.**
Pressing the Esc key returns you to the DOS Shell screen.

REVIEW

1 Start the DOS Shell.

2 If necessary, press **Tab** to move to the Directory Tree window; then select the directory that contains the file you want to display.

3 Press **Tab** to move to the file list window.

4 Use ↑ or ↓ to highlight the file you want to display.

5 Press **Alt** to activate the menu bar.

6 Type **F** to open the File menu.

7 Type **V** to select the View File Contents command.

8 Press **Esc** to quit the display.

SHORTCUT

You also can press the F9 key to select the View File Contents command.

Search for a file

```
                          MS-DOS Shell
 File  Options  View  Tree  Help
C:\
   A      B      C

          Directory Tree                        C:\*.*
    C:\                    Search File                    247    06-28-91  ↑
      123                                              47,867    03-08-91
      AFT    Current Directory is C:\                     256    06-25-91
      AMI                                               1,797    08-07-91
      COL    Search for. .   *.*_                          50    07-26-90
      DOS                                              11,304    05-01-90
      EXC          [X] Search entire disk              94,208    09-05-91
      EZD                                              94,208    09-05-91
      EZF                                              11,845    06-06-91
      FON                                              73,612    06-06-91
      HG3      ( OK )      ( Cancel )      ( Help )      1,883    09-05-91
      MOU                                                 128    01-29-91
      NORTON                           WINA20  .386     9,349    03-08-91
      PCFILE                                                               ↓
                              Main
    Command Prompt                                                         ↑
    Editor
    MS-DOS QBasic
    Disk Utilities


 F10=Actions   Shift+F9=Command Prompt                             10:18a
```

Oops!

If the search does not find the requested file, you see the message `No files match file specifier`. Press the Esc key and try the search again. You may have typed the name incorrectly.

 Start the DOS Shell.
For help with this step, see *TASK: Start the DOS Shell*. If the DOS Shell is already started, skip this step.

2 **Press Alt.**
Pressing the Alt key activates the menu bar.

 Type F.
This step opens the File menu.

4 **Type h.**
This step selects the Search command. You see the Search File dialog box. The Search for text box contains *.*; the cursor is positioned inside this box. Also notice the check box marked `Search entire disk`. When the check box contains an X, the DOS Shell looks everywhere on your disk for the file. (The Before screen shows this step.)

5 **Type AUTOEXEC.*.**
This step tells the DOS Shell to find all files with any extension and the name AUTOEXEC.

 Press Enter.
Pressing Enter confirms the name and starts the search. The DOS Shell looks through all directories for files that match this name. When it finds a file, a window appears with the words `Search Results for: AUTOEXEC.*`. You see the location of all matching files.

After

```
                        MS-DOS Shell
  File  Options  View  Tree  Help
                  Search Results for: AUTOEXEC.*
  ▤ C:\AUTOEXEC.BAT                                    ↑
  ▤ C:\UTIL\AUTOEXEC.BAT






                              ▷









                                                       ↓
  F10=Actions   Esc=Cancel                       10:18a
```

7 **Press** Esc.
Pressing the Esc key closes the Search Results window.

REVIEW

1 Start the DOS Shell.

2 Press **Alt** to activate the menu bar.

3 Type **F** to open the File menu.

4 Type **h** to select the Search command.

5 Type the file name you want to find. You can use wild cards.

6 Press **Enter**.

7 Press **Esc** to close the Search Results window.

Note

A wild card is a character that matches any character or characters. The question mark wild card (?) matches a single character. The asterisk wild card (*) matches all characters.

Create a directory

```
                          MS-DOS Shell
 File  Options  View  Tree  Help
 C:\
 ▭A   ▭B   ▬C
          Directory Tree                        C:\*.*
 ┌─ C:\                          ↑  │ ▭ AUTOEXEC.BAT    247    06-28-91 ↑
 │  ├─ 123R23                       │ ▭ COMMAND .COM  47,867   03-08-91
 │  ├─ AFTERDRK                     │ ▭ CONFIG  .SYS     256   06-25-91
 │  ├─ AMIPRO                       │ ▭ DEFAULT .BAK   1,797   08-07-91
 │  ├─ COLLAGE                      │ ▭ FONTWID .BAT      50   07-26-90
 │  ├─ DOS                          │ ▭ HIMEM   .SYS  11,304   05-01-90
 │  ├─ EXCEL                        │ ▭ IMAGE   .BAK  94,208   09-05-91
 │  ├─ EZDFIGS                      │ ▭ IMAGE   .DAT  94,208   09-05-91
 │  ├─ EZFIGS                       │ ▭ NDOS    .COM  11,845   06-06-91
 │  ├─ FONTS                        │ ▭ NDOS    .OVL  73,612   06-06-91
 │  ├─ HG3                          │ ▭ TREEINFO.NCD   1,883   09-05-91
 │  ├─ MOUSE1                       │ ▭ VP      .BAT     128   01-29-91
 │  ├─ NORTON                       │ ▭ WINA20  .386   9,349   03-08-91
 │  ├─ PCFILE                    ↓  │                                 ↓
                               Main
 ▭ Command Prompt                                                    ↑
 ▭ Editor
 ▭ MS-DOS QBasic
 ▭ Disk Utilities



                                                                    ↓
 F10=Actions  Shift+F9=Command Prompt                       10:18a
```

Oops!

Be sure to select the directory that will contain the new directory first. Remember that you are creating the directory within the current directory.

1 **Start the DOS Shell.**
For help with this step, see *TASK: Start the DOS Shell*. If the DOS Shell is already started, skip this step.

2 **Press Tab to move to the Directory Tree window.**
This step moves you to the Directory Tree window so that you can create a directory.

3 **Be sure that the root directory (C:\) is selected.**
You will create a directory that is a subdirectory of the root directory. If you want to place the new directory within another directory, select that directory first.

4 **Press Alt.**
Pressing the Alt key activates the menu bar.

5 **Type F.**
This step opens the File menu. You see a list of File commands.

6 **Type e.**
This step selects the Create Directory command. You see the Create Directory dialog box. This dialog box lists the current directory name (called the Parent name) and contains a New directory name text box.

7 **Type MEMOS.**
MEMOS is the name of the directory that you want to create.

After

Note

To remove a directory, see *TASK: Remove a directory*.

8 **Press Enter.**

Pressing Enter confirms the name and creates the directory. The new directory is selected. The After screen shows the new directory.

REVIEW

1 Start the DOS Shell.

2 Press **Tab** to move to the Directory Tree window.

3 Use ↑ or ↓ to select the directory that will contain the new directory.

4 Press **Alt** to activate the menu bar.

5 Type **F** to open the File menu.

6 Type **e** to select the Create Directory command.

7 Type the directory name.

8 Press **Enter**.

Note

If you type a directory name that already exists, you see a message stating that access is denied. Type **2** and press **Enter**; then try again. Use a different name this time.

Remove a directory

```
                         MS-DOS Shell
 File  Options  View  Tree  Help
C:\MEMOS
 ⊟A   ⊟B   ▭C
┌───────Directory Tree───────┐┌──────C:\MEMOS\*.*──────┐
│  ┌─ C:\                    ▲││    No files in selected directory.  ▲│
│  ├─⊞ 123R23        ▷       ││                         │
│  ├─⊞ AFTERDRK              ││                         │
│  ├─⊞ AMIPRO                ││                         │
│  ├─⊡ COLLAGE               ││                         │
│  ├─⊞ DOS                   ││                         │
│  ├─⊞ EXCEL                 ││                         │
│  ├─⊡ EZDFIGS               ││                         │
│  ├─⊞ EZFIGS                ││                         │
│  ├─⊡ FONTS                 ││                         │
│  ├─⊞ HG3                   ││                         │
│  ├─⊡ MEMOS                 ││                         │
│  ├─⊡ MOUSE1                ││                         │
│  └─⊡ NORTON              ▼ ││                        ▼│
├──────────────────Main──────────────────┤
│ ▭ Command Prompt                        ▲│
│ ▭ Editor                                 │
│ ▭ MS-DOS QBasic                          │
│ ▦ Disk Utilities                         │
│                                         ▼│
 F10=Actions   Shift+F9=Command Prompt          10:18a
```

Oops!

If you change your mind and do not want to remove the directory, press the Esc key in the Delete Directory Confirmation box.

1 **Start the DOS Shell.**
For help with this step, see *TASK: Start the DOS Shell*. If the DOS Shell is already started, skip this step.

2 **Press Tab to move to the Directory Tree window.**
This step moves you to the Directory Tree window so that you can remove a directory.

3 **Press ↑ or ↓ until you highlight the MEMOS directory.**
MEMOS is the directory that you want to delete. If you don't have this directory, select one that you do have. Be sure to select one that you don't need.

The MEMOS directory should be empty. If not, you may want to create an empty directory for this exercise. (See *TASK: Create a directory*.) You cannot remove a directory unless all the files in that directory are deleted.

4 **Press Alt.**
Pressing the Alt key activates the menu bar.

5 **Type F.**
This step opens the File menu. You see a list of File commands.

6 **Type D.**
This step selects the Delete command. You see the Delete Directory Confirmation alert box.

After

```
                          MS-DOS Shell
 File  Options  View  Tree  Help
 C:\HG3
 ▭A    ▭B    ▬C

        Directory Tree                    C:\HG3\*.*
 ┌─ C:\                          ↑  ▦ 640X350 .B&W       18,726  04-06-91 ↑
 │  ┌┬ 123R23              ▓         ▦ 640X350 .CLR       25,164  04-06-91
 │  ├┬ AFTERDRK               ▦ 640X480 .CLR       30,912  04-06-91
 │  ├┬ AMIPRO                 □ AGXCOM  .EXE       41,904  01-21-91
 │  ├─ COLLAGE                □ CAPTURE .EXE       25,357  01-09-91
 │  ├┬ DOS                    □ CH3TOCHT.EXE       40,697  04-05-91
 │  ├┬ EXCEL                  ▦ EGALOGO .PCX       58,766  01-28-91
 │  ├─ EZDFIGS                ▦ HG3     .CF3        3,553  05-17-91
 │  ├┬ EZFIGS                 ▦ HG3     .ERR       25,857  04-05-91
 │  ├─ FONTS                  ▦ HG3     .EXE       77,458  04-10-91
 │  ├┬ HG3                    ▦ HG3     .FGF       12,942  04-05-91
 │  ├─ MOUSE1                 ▦ HG3     .HLP      180,294  04-05-91
 │  ├─ NORTON                 ▦ HG3     .ICO          766  12-20-90
 │  └─ PCFILE              ↓  ▦ HG3     .OVL    1,429,313  04-10-91 ↓
                          Main
 □ Command Prompt                                                      ↑
 □ Editor
 □ MS-DOS QBasic
 ▦ Disk Utilities




 F10=Actions  Shift+F9=Command Prompt                          10:18a ↓
```

7   **Press Enter.**
Pressing Enter confirms that you want to delete the directory.

REVIEW

1   Start the DOS Shell.

2   Press **Tab** to move to the Directory Tree window.

3   Use ↑ and ↓ to select the directory that you want to remove.

4   Press **Alt** to activate the menu bar.

5   Type **F** to open the File menu.

6   Type **D** to select the Delete command.

7   Press **Enter** to confirm the deletion.

Note

If the directory contains files or other directories, you see a Deletion Error alert box telling you that you cannot delete a directory that is not empty. Delete all files and subdirectories in the directory and then try again.

Reference

- Quick Reference

- Error Messages

- Software Guide

- Glossary

Quick Reference

Task	Command
Change directories	CD
Change the date	DATE
Change the time	TIME
Change the volume label	LABEL
Clear the screen	CLS
Copy a disk	DISKCOPY
Copy a file	COPY
Create a directory	MD
Delete a file	DEL
Display a directory	DIR
Display a file's contents	TYPE
Display available disk space	CHKDSK
Display available RAM	MEM (DOS 5, 6, and 6.2)
Display DOS version	VER
Format a disk	FORMAT
Remove a directory	RD
Rename a file	RENAME
Restore files	RESTORE
Set the system prompt	PROMPT

Error Messages

This guide contains some of the error messages that you might run across and explains what to do when you receive them.

Abort, Retry, Fail?

You might get this message when you are trying to access a disk drive. The message might mean that the disk is not formatted, the disk is bad, or the disk is not inserted properly. Eject and reinsert the disk and try typing **R**. If this doesn't work, type **F** to fail. Or type **A** to abort (cancel) the operation.

You are prompted `Current drive is no longer valid` if you type **F** to fail. Type **C:** and press **Enter** to return to drive C.

All files will be deleted

When you type **DEL** *.*, you tell DOS to delete everything in the directory. This command could be dangerous if you don't intend to delete every file in the directory. This message allows you to confirm the deleting (type **Y**) or cancel the command (type **N**).

Bad command or file name

When you type a command that DOS does not recognize, you see the message `Bad command or file name`. You might have simply typed the command incorrectly (such as typing DES instead of DEL). Check your typing and try the command again.

Duplicate file name or file not found

If you used RENAME and typed, as the new name, a name that already exists, you see this message. You also see this message if you used RENAME and typed, as the original file name, a file that doesn't exist. Check the command and try again.

File cannot be copied to itself

If you type the COPY command and don't tell DOS the name of the copy, you receive this error message. Type the command again, but this time specify the name of the file you want to create (the new copy).

File not found

If you try to access a file that is not in the current directory (or not in the path), or if you type the file name incorrectly, you get this message. Check your typing and try again, or change to the correct directory and try again.

Insufficient disk space

To copy a file to another disk, that disk must have enough space for the file (or files). If the disk doesn't contain enough space, you get this message. Erase any unneeded files and try again.

Non-System disk or disk error

When DOS starts, it usually looks for certain files. Usually it starts by looking on drive A for these files. If a disk is inserted into drive A, and it is not a system disk (DOS has not been added to it), you see this message. Eject the disk and press any key to continue.

Other Errors

See *Using MS-DOS 6.2,* Special Edition, for information on other errors you might receive.

Software Guide

To use your computer to perform specific tasks (writing a letter, balancing a budget, storing real estate clients), you need to purchase and install applications. *Applications* are tools you use on the computer. A computer doesn't really perform unless you add different applications (also called *programs* or *software*).

This guide discusses the most common categories of applications, briefly explains what each type does, and lists a few representative software packages. For more information, see *Introduction to Personal Computers,* 4th Edition, (published by Que) or pick up any personal computing magazine (such as *PC World*, *PCWeek*, *PC Magazine*) and read the ads. If you need help with a particular application, Que publishes titles on most of the popular software packages.

Types of Applications

There are basically 10 categories of applications:

- Word processors

- Spreadsheets

- Databases

- Graphics

- Desktop publishing

- Communication

- Integrated programs

- Financial

- Education

- Games

This software guide discusses each type of category.

A Word about Windows

Microsoft Windows is a graphical user interface. It is designed to be an interface between the user and DOS. (You still need DOS.) Rather than memorize and type commands, you access commands through the menus. Microsoft Windows helps you manage files and run programs.

Some programs are designed specifically to work with Microsoft Windows. These programs work essentially in the same way. That is, after you learn one Windows program, you can easily learn other Windows programs. Some Windows programs are noted in the following sections. To use these programs, you must have Microsoft Windows.

Word Processors

You use word processors to create memos, letters, reports, brochures, and other printed material. A word processor is like a typewriter—but much better.

Most word processors offer several features that let you work with text easily. You can complete these tasks:

See text as you type on-screen. Because the text is not committed to paper, you can make changes and corrections—delete text, add text, and so on.

Rearrange text. As you write, you might decide that the last paragraph really belongs in the introduction. With a word processor, you can move the text from one spot to another. This process is called *cut and paste*.

Spell check your document. Nothing mars a document worse than a glaring typo or misspelled word. Most word processors offer a speller. You can check the spelling of your document before you print.

Save the document. You can save the document on disk and use it again.

Format the document. Word processors vary in the formatting features they offer. Simple word processors enable you to set tabs, change margins, and select different fonts or font styles (bold, italic, and so on). Complex word processors include these features, but they also allow you to add footers and headers, create columns, insert graphics, and so on.

The most common word processing programs are

- Ami Pro (available only for Windows)

- Microsoft Word for DOS

- Microsoft Word for Windows

- Professional Write

- WordPerfect

- WordPerfect for Windows

- WordStar

The following is a screen from Ami Pro:

The following is a screen from WordPerfect:

File	Edit	View	Layout	Tools	Font	Graphics	Window	Help

| Marg ▼ | None ▼ | 1 Col ▼ | Left ▼ | CG Times ▼ | 12pt ▼ |

| File Mgr | Save As | Print | Preview | Font | GrphMode | TextMode | Envelope | Speller | Gramatik | QuikFndr | Tbl Edit | Search |

CG Times 12pt   Doc 1 Pg 1 Ln 1" Pos 1"

Spreadsheets

A *spreadsheet* is an electronic version of an accountant's pad. You use a spreadsheet program to set up *worksheets*. Worksheets can total sales by division, keep track of a monthly budget, calculate loan balances, and perform other financial analysis.

With a spreadsheet program, you can complete these tasks:

Calculate formulas. You can write simple formulas to add, subtract, multiply, and divide. You can depend on the spreadsheet program to calculate the results correctly every time.

Change data and recalculate. You can change, add, or delete data, and then recalculate the results automatically. You never have to erase and rewrite when you forget a crucial figure. And you don't have to recalculate all the amounts manually when you do make a change or an addition.

Rearrange data. With your worksheet on-screen, you can add or delete a column or row. You can copy and move data from one spot to another.

Repeat information. You can copy text, a value, or a formula to another place in the worksheet. In your monthly budget worksheet, for example, you total the expenses for each month. You could write a formula that calculates January's totals, and you then could copy this formula for February through December.

Change the format of data. You can format your results in many ways. You can display a number with dollar signs, as a percent, or as a date. You can align text left, right, or center.

Print data. You can print reports of your data.

Create charts. Most spreadsheet programs allow you to graph your data and print that graph. You can create pie graphs, bar graphs, line graphs, and many other graph types.

The most common spreadsheet programs are

- Lotus 1-2-3

- Lotus 1-2-3 for Windows

- Lotus Improv

- Microsoft Excel (available for Windows)

- Quattro Pro

- Quattro Pro for Windows

The following is a screen from Lotus 1-2-3:

The following is a screen from Microsoft Excel:

Databases

A *database* is similar to a complex card file. You store related information together. For example, you can use a database to keep track of real estate clients, a baseball card collection, employees, inventory—any set of data.

Each piece of data, such as a phone number, is stored in a *field*. A set of fields makes up a *record*, such as a name, address, and phone number. A *database* is a collection of all the records.

With a database, you can complete these tasks:

Retrieve data. After you enter data, you can retrieve it easily. Rather than sift through several paper documents, you can quickly pull up the data on-screen—for instance, an invoice.

Sort data. You can rearrange data. For example, you might want an alphabetical list of clients sorted by last name to use as a phone list. You might want to sort the same list by ZIP code to do a mailing.

Print data. You can print reports, mailing labels, and other output.

Some of the most common database packages include

- Microsoft Access

- dBASE

- FileMaker Pro

- Microsoft FoxPro

- Paradox

- Paradox for Windows

- Personal R:BASE

- Q&A

The following is a screen from Paradox:

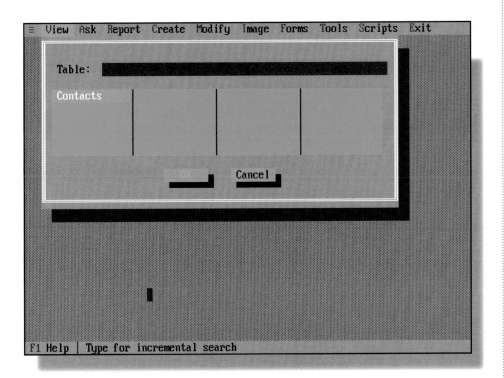

Graphics

With graphics programs, you can create simple to complex illustrations. This category also includes presentation programs, which enable you to create graphs, and computer-aided design (CAD) programs, which enable you to create architectural and other complex drawings.

With graphics programs, you can do the following:

Use many drawing tools. The tools offered by packages vary. You can draw geometric shapes (such as circles, squares, rectangles, and lines), add fills and color, add text, trace objects, align objects, and so on.

Edit drawings. If you don't get the drawing just right, you can modify it. You can delete parts of the drawing and redraw them.

Create drawings to be used over and over. You might, for instance, create a logo that you can use on hundreds of company documents.

Programs in this category include

- AutoCAD (CAD)

- CorelDRAW! (draw)

- Freelance Graphics (presentation)

- Generic CADD (CAD)

- Harvard Graphics (presentation)

- PC Paintbrush (draw)

- PowerPoint (charts; available for Windows)

- Windows Paintbrush

- WordPerfect Presentation

The following is a screen from Windows Paintbrush:

The following is a screen from Harvard Graphics:

Desktop Publishing

Desktop publishing programs enable you to create sophisticated brochures, newsletters, fliers, resumes, menus, reports, and other output. Some word processing packages offer desktop publishing capabilities (such as column layout), but the features offered by desktop publishing programs are more sophisticated. Keep in mind that if you do use a desktop publishing program, you also will probably use a word processor to create the text.

With a desktop publishing program, you can complete the following tasks:

Lay out a page. With a desktop publishing program, you have precise control over the layout of the page—the margins, headers, footers, and so on. You also have control over the text—what font, size, and style are used; where the text is placed; and how the text flows.

Change page layout. If you don't like how the document looks, you can experiment with the layout until you get the document just the way you want it.

Create templates. You can create a template for a document that you create over and over—such as a newsletter. The headings and layout would be set—you just have to add the text.

The most popular desktop publishing packages are

- Microsoft Publisher

- PageMaker

- PFS: First Publisher

- QuarkXpress

- Ventura Publisher

The following is a screen from PageMaker:

Communication

Communication programs enable you to use your computer to talk to other computers. You might, for example, need to access a huge computer (called a *mainframe*) that stores stock figures so that you can get up-to-the-minute reports. Or you might need some sales data from your district office's computer. With a communication program, you can send and receive information over the phone lines.

You also can connect to on-line services (such as GEnie or CompuServe) that enable you to shop, leave messages for other users, play games with other users (even users in other countries!), download programs, and so on.

To use your computer to communicate, you must also have a modem and a phone line. (For more information on modems, see *Introduction to Personal Computers,* 4th Edition, or *Introduction to PC Communication*, published by Que.) You also need a communication package. PROCOMM PLUS and CrossTalk are examples of this type of package.

Integrated Programs

Integrated programs combine several types of programs into one package: word processing, database, spreadsheet, and communications. Each program offers the benefits previously discussed. Integrated programs also have the added benefit of allowing you to integrate the data from one program to the next. For example, you can use the mailing list from your database to personalize form letters with your word processor. You can copy financial figures from the spreadsheet to a report in the word processor. On the downside, each of the programs will not offer as many features as "stand-alone" or dedicated packages.

Here are some examples of this type of program:

- ClarisWorks

- Enable/OA

- GeoWorks

- LotusWorks

- Microsoft Works

- PFS: WindowWorks (available for Windows)

- PFS:First Choice

- WordPerfect Works

The following is a screen from GeoWorks:

Financial Programs

Financial programs enable you to create tax returns, balance your checkbook, set up an accounting system, and perform other finance-related tasks. These programs range from the simple to the complex. Some examples are

- Managing Your Money (simple check-writing program; also can be used for limited accounting purposes)

- Peachtree (complete accounting package—general ledger, accounts receivable, accounts payable, payroll)

- Quicken

- Quicken for Windows

- TurboTax (tax preparation program)

The following is a screen from Quicken:

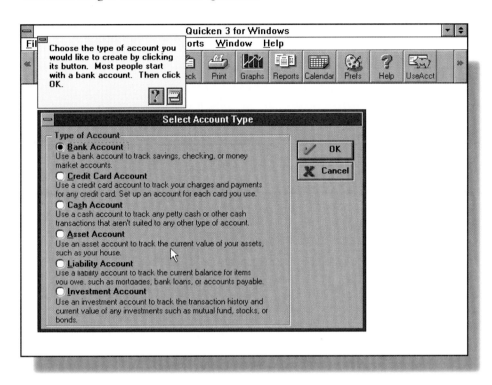

Education

Personal computers are easy to use, which makes them ideal for learning new tasks. You can use programs to learn to type, master a foreign language, plan a travel route for a trip, and accomplish many other educational tasks.

Games

Last but not least, you can use the computer to play games. Games can range from playing on-screen card games (Solitaire) to diagnosing and performing surgery on a patient (Life and Death) to playing golf (Mean 18 Ultimate Golf) to flying a plane (Flight Simulator).

The following is a screen from Solitaire:

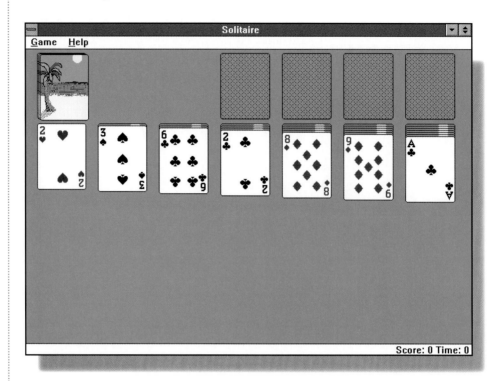

Others

Not all programs fit into a neat category. New programs are created every day. Programs are available that enable you to draw up a will, create a calendar, complete complex statistical analyses, and calculate calories. Just browse through some of the computer magazines (*PC World* or *PC Week*, for example) to get an idea of the world of possibilities. Explore with your computer. Be productive. But most of all, have fun.

Glossary

application   A computer program used for a particular task—such as word processing. In most cases, *program*, *software*, and *application* mean the same thing and can be used interchangeably.

AUTOEXEC.BAT   A file that DOS executes when you start the computer. This file may include commands that control different settings. You might, for example, include a PATH command that tells DOS where your programs are located.

backup   A copy of data or programs that you make in case the original data or program becomes damaged.

batch file   A file that contains a series of DOS commands. The commands are executed when you run the batch file. You might create a batch file that changes to a certain directory and starts a program, for example.

boot   The process of starting a computer.

byte   A measure of the amount of information that is equal to about one character.

capacity   A term used to describe how much data you can store on a disk. Capacity is measured in kilobytes (K) or megabytes (M).

COMMAND.COM   An essential DOS file that contains the command processor.

CONFIG.SYS   A special file that sets configuration settings. DOS consults this file when started. Some applications require that special commands be in the CONFIG.SYS file.

cursor   A marker used to indicate the current position on-screen.

defragment   A method of rearranging the information on your hard disk so that files are stored in contiguous sections. Defragmenting a disk can improve (speed up) the performance of the disk.

density   A term used to describe the amount of information you can store on a floppy disk. Double-density disks store 360 kilobytes or 720 kilobytes of data; high-density disks store 1.2 megabytes or 1.44 megabytes of data.

directory   An index to the files stored on disk or a list of files. A directory is similar to a file cabinet; you can group files together in directories.

DOS   Acronym for *disk operating system*. DOS manages the details of your system—storing and retrieving programs and files.

DOS prompt   The indicator you see on-screen (for instance, C:>) that tells you DOS is ready for a command.

file   The various individual reports, memos, databases, and letters that you store on your hard drive (or floppy disk) for future use.

file name   The name you assign a file when you store it to disk. A file name consists of two parts: the root and the extension. The root can be up to eight characters in length. The extension can be up to three characters long and usually indicates the file type. The root and extension are separated by a period. SALES.DOC is a valid file name. SALES is the root, and DOC is the extension.

file spec   The combination of file name and extension, usually with the use of wild cards. The file spec *.DOC means all files with the DOC extension. The file spec MEMO.* means all files named MEMO with any extension.

floppy disk   A storage device. Floppy disks come in two sizes (3 1/2-inch and 5 1/4-inch), two densities (double-density and high-density), and different capacities. (5 1/4-inch disks can store either 360 kilobytes or 1.2 megabytes. 3 1/2-inch disks can store either 720 kilobytes or 1.44 megabytes.)

floppy disk drive   A device that reads (retrieves) and writes (stores) information on a floppy disk.

format   The process that prepares a disk for use.

hard disk   A data storage device. Hard disks vary in size—they can range from 20 megabytes to over 155 megabytes. They also vary in type. Some hard disks are encased in the system unit. You also can have an external hard disk that is outside the system unit.

hardware   The physical parts of the computer—the screen, the keyboard, the mouse, and so on.

kilobyte (K)   About one thousand (1,024) bytes. Kilobytes measure disk capacity.

megabyte (M)   One million bytes of information. Megabytes measure disk capacity.

monitor   The piece of hardware that displays on-screen what you type on the keyboard.

mouse   A pointing device used in some programs to move the mouse pointer on-screen, select windows, and issue commands.

path   The route, through directories, to a program or document file. The path C:\REPORTS\SALES\EASTDIV.DOC, for example, includes five elements: the disk drive (C:); the root directory (\); the directory (REPORTS); the subdirectory, which is a directory within the first directory (SALES); and the file name (EASTDIV.DOC).

program   A set of instructions that tells a computer what to do. *Program* means the same as *application* or *software*.

RAM   An acronym for *random-access memory*. A temporary place where the computer stores data and program instructions.

restore   The procedure used to copy backup files back to the hard disk. Because backup files are stored in a special format, you must use a special restore program to restore the files to their original format.

root directory   The main directory. All other directories branch off the root directory.

shell   A program that acts as a user interface to the features of an operating system.

software   Another term for computer programs or applications. You run software on your hardware.

subdirectory   A list of files or an index to the files stored on disk. A directory is similar to a file cabinet; you can group files together in directories. *Subdirectory* means the same as *directory*.

syntax   The format and rules you follow when issuing a command.

virus   A program that carries out unwanted and sometimes damaging procedures on your computer.

wild card   A character used to represent other characters. A question mark (?) wild card matches any single character. An asterisk (*) wild card matches any number of characters.

Index

Symbols

PG (Display current directory), 37-39
* (asterisk) wild card, 191
? (qustion mark) wild card, 191
3 1/2-inch floppy disks, 13-14
5 1/4-inch floppy disks, 13-14

A

Abort, Retry, Fail? error message, 198
All files will be deleted error message, 199
Alt key, 16-17
Alt-B (previous topic) key combination, 42-43
Alt-F (File menu) key combination, 46-47
Alt-S (Search menu) key combination, 44-45
Ami Pro word processing program, 202
anti-virus programs, MSAV, 123-127
applications, *see* programs
arrow keys, 16-17
AutoCAD (CAD) graphics program, 208
AUTOEXEC.BAT file, 22-23, 32-35, 215
   prompt statements, 39
AUTOEXEC.UMB file, 147

B

backslash (\), 19
Backspace key, 16
backups, 104-111, 215
   directories, 112-115
   exiting Microsoft Backup, 122
   files, 116-119
   restoring,120-121, 217
Bad command or file name error message, 48-58, 60-61, 130, 136, 199
batch files, 215
booting computers, 18, 34-35, 215
buttons, Reset, 34-35
bytes, 215

C

capacity of disks, 215
CD command, 56-61, 198
CHKDSK command, 136-137, 198
ClarisWork integrated program, 211
clearing screens, 50-51
CLS command, 50-51, 198
Collapse Branch command (DOS Shell), 164-165
Collapse Directory (-, minus) shortcut key, 165
collapsing directories in DOS Shell, 164-165
COMMAND.COM file, 22-23, 215
commands, 25
   CD, 56- 61, 198
   CHKDSK, 136-137, 198
   CLS, 50-51, 198
   COPY, 86-89, 198
   DATE, 138-139, 198
   DEFRAG, 148-149
   DEL, 96-99, 198
   DIR, 48-49, 52-53, 62-69, 198
   DISKCOPY, 78-81, 198
   DOSSHELL, 152-153
   Exit, 46-47
   Find, 44-45
   FORMAT, 74-75, 198
   HELP, 40- 45
   LABEL, 132-133, 198
   MD, 54-55, 198
   MEM, 144-145, 198
   MEMMAKER, 146-147
   MSAV, 123-125
   MSBACKUP, 104-111
   PATH, 22, 142-143
   PROMPT, 37-39, 198
   RD, 62-63, 198
   RENAME, 94-95, 198
   RESTORE, 198
   Syntax, 217
   TIME, 140-141, 198
   TREE, 60-61
   TYPE, 84-85, 198
   UNDELETE, 100-101
   VER, 134-135
   VERF, 198

VOL, 130-131
VSAFE, 126-127
commands (DOS Shell)
    Collapse Branch, 164-165
    Expand Branch, 162-163
    File menu
        Copy, 180-181
        Create Directory, 192-193
        Delete, 186-187, 194-195
        Exit, 154-157
        Move, 184-185
        Rename, 182-183
        Search, 190-191
        Select All, 178-179
        View, 188-189
    Help, 158-159
    Options menu, File Display, 170-173
    Tree menu, Expand All, 166-167
communications programs, 210-211
compare process, backups, 110
computers, 12-13
    booting,18, 215
    care and maintenance, 25
    rebooting, 34-35
    setting date/time, 32, 138-141
    starting, 32-33
    turning off, 36
    viruses, 123-127, 217
CONFIG.SYS file, 32-35, 215
CONFIG.UMB file, 147
configuring Microsoft Backup, 106-111
conventional memory, 144
COPY command, 86-89, 198
Copy command (DOS Shell File
        menu), 180-181
copying
    files, 86-87
        all files to new drive, 92-93
        DOS Shell, 180-181
        groups, 90-91
        to another directory, 88-89
    floppy disks, 78-81
CorelDRAW! (draw) graphics
        program, 208
Create Directory command (DOS Shell
        File menu), 192-193
Ctrl key, 16-17
Ctrl-Alt-Del key, rebooting computers,
        34-35
cursors, 215

D

database programs, 206
DATE command, 138-139, 198
dates/times, 32
    setting, 138-141
dBASE database program, 206
defaults, DOS prompt, 37-39
DEFRAG command, 148-149
defragmenting hard disks, 148-149,
        215
DEL command, 96-99, 198
Del key, 16-17
Delete command (DOS Shell File
        menu), 186-187, 194-195
deleting
    directories, 62-63
        DOS Shell, 194-195
    files, 63, 96-97
        all files, 98-99
        DOS Shell, 186-187
        undeleting, 100-101
Deletion Error alert box, 195
density of floppy disks, 215
desktop publishing programs, 209-210
dimmed commands, 155
DIR command, 48-49, 52-53, 62-69,
        198
directories, 18-19, 215
    backups, 112-115
    changing, 56-59
    collapsing in DOS Shell, 164-165
    copying files between, 88-89
    creating, 54-55
    deleting, 62-63
    displaying, 37-39, 68-69
    DOS Shell
        creating, 192-193
        deleting, 194-195
        expanding, 162-163, 166-167
    files, 48-49
        listing, 52-53, 93
    paths, 142-143, 217
Directory already exists error
        message, 54
Directory Tree window, 153, 160-161,
        172-173
directory trees, 60-61
Directory window, displaying files,
        170-171

disk drives, 14
  changing, 76-77
  floppy, 12, 216
    testing, 106-107
  inserting floppy disks, 72-73
  selecting DOS Shell, 168-169
  see also floppy disks; hard disks
disk operating system, *see* DOS
displaying file contents, 84-85
DISKCOPY command, 78-81, 198
DOS
  prompt, 36-39, 216
  starting, 32-33
  versions, 23, 134-135
DOS Shell, 23-24
  directories
    collapsing, 164-165
    creating, 192-193
    deleting, 194-195
    expanding, 162-163, 166-167
  disk drives, 168-169
  exiting, 156-157
  files
    copying, 180-181
    deleting, 186-187
    displaying, 160-161, 170-171
    finding, 190-191
    moving, 184-185
    renaming, 182-183
    selecting, 174-179
    sorting, 172-173
    viewing, 188-189
  Help menu, 158-159
  menus, 154-155
  starting, 152-153
DOSSHELL command, 152-153
drive icon area, DOS Shell, 153
drives, copying all files, 92-93
Duplicate file name or file not found error message, 199

E

education programs, 213
Enable/OA integrated program, 211
End, 16
Enhanced keyboard, 17
Enter key, 16, 18

error messages
  Abort, Retry, Fail?, 198
  All files will be deleted, 199
  Bad command or file name, 48-53, 58, 60-61, 130, 136, 199
  Directory already exists, 54
  Duplicate file name or file not found, 199
  File cannot be copied to itself, 86-87, 199
  File not found, 66, 85
  Insufficient disk space, 199
  Invalid directory, 56
  Invalid Switch, 59
  Non-System disk or disk error, 199
  Non-System disk or disk error. Replace and press any key when ready, 33
  Not Ready reading drive A. Abort, Retry, Fail?, 76-77
  Press any key to continue, 64
  Too many parameters, 67-68
Excel (Microsoft) spreadsheet program, 204
Exit command (DOS Shell File menu), 46-47, 154-157
exiting
  DOS Shell, 156-157
  Microsoft Backup, 122
  programs, 36
Expand All command (DOS Shell Tree menu), 166-167
Expand Branch command (DOS Shell), 162-163
Expand Directory (*, asterisk) shortcut key, 163
Expand Directory (+, plus) shortcut key, 163
expanded memory, 144
expanding directories in DOS Shell, 162-163, 166-167
extended memory, 144
extensions, file names, 20-21
  sorting by, 172-173

F

File cannot be copied to itself
    error message, 86-87, 199
File not found error message, 85
File Copy (F8) shortcut key, 181
File Delete (Del) shortcut key, 187
File Display command (DOS Shell
    Options menu), 170-173
File Exit (Alt-F4) key combination, 157
File Exit (Alt-F4) shortcut key, 157
file list, 153
    selecting files, 174-179
file names, 20-21, 216
    extensions, 48-49
    sorting by, 172-173
File not found error message, 66
file specs, 216
FileMaker Pro database program, 206
files, 18-19, 216
    AUTOEXEC.BAT, 22-23, 32-35,
      215
      prompt statements, 39
    AUTOEXEC.UMB, 147
    backups, 104-111, 116-119
    COMMAND.COM, 22-23, 215
    CONFIG.SYS, 32-35, 215
    CONFIG.UMB, 147
    copying, 86-87
      all files to new drive, 92-93
      groups, 90-91
      in DOS Shell, 180-181
      to another directory, 88-89
    defragmenting, 215
    deleting, 63, 96-97
      all files, 98-99
      undeleting, 100-101
    displaying, 48-49, 66-67, 84-85
    DOS Shell, 186-187
      displaying, 160-161, 170-171
      moving, 184-185
      finding, 190-191
      renaming, 182-183
      selecting, 174-179
      viewing, 188-189
      wide listing, 52-53
    listing, pausing, 64-65
    renaming, 94-95

restoring, 120-121, 217
    sorting, 172-173
    undeleting, 100-101
financial programs, 212
Find command, 44-45
Find dialog box, 44-45
finding files
    DOS Shell, 190-191
    Help topics, 44-45
floppy disks, 12-14, 216
    care and maintenance, 25
    copying, 78-81
    formatting, 74-75, 216
    inserting, 72-73
    selecting drives, 168-169
    testing drives, 106-107
FORMAT command, 74-75, 198
formatting disks, 216
    floppy, 74-75
    hard, 216
Freelance Graphics (presentation)
    graphics program, 208
function keys, 16-17

G–H

games, 213
Generic CADD (CAD) graphics
    program, 208
GeoWorks integrated program, 211
graphics programs, 207-208
groups, files, copying, 90-91

hard disks, 12-13, 15
    backups, 104-111
    defragmenting, 148-149
    formatting, 216
    memory, 136-137
hardware, 216
    care and maintenance, 25
Harvard Graphics (presentation)
    graphics program, 208
Help
    commands, Exit, 46-47
    DOS Shell, 158-159
    finding topics, 44-45
HELP command, 40-45
Home key, 16

I

Ins key, 16-17
inserting floppy disks, 72-73
Insufficient disk space error
        message, 199
integrated programs, 211
Invalid directory error message, 56
Invalid Switch error message, 59

K–L

key combinations
    Alt-B (previous topic), 42-43
    Alt-F (File menu), 46-47
    Alt-N (Display next topic), 42-43
    Alt-S (Search menu), 44-45
    File Exit (Alt-F4), 157
    see also shortcut keys
keyboards, 15-18
kilobyte (K), 216

LABEL command, 132-133, 198
listing directories, 93
Lotus 1-2-3 for Windows spreadsheet
        program, 204
Lotus 1-2-3 spreadsheet program, 204
Lotus Improv spreadsheet program,
        204
LotusWorks integrated program, 211

M

Managing Your Money financial
        program, 212
MD command, 54-55, 198
megabyte (M), 216
MEM command, 144-145, 198
MEMMAKER command, 146-147
memory, 144-145
    hard disks, 136-137
    optimizing, 146-147
menus, 154-155
Microsoft programs
    Excel spreadsheet, 204
    Windows, 201
    Windows Paintbrush, 208
    word processing

        Word for DOS, 202
        Word for Windows, 202
Microsoft Access database program,
        206
Microsoft Backup, 104-105, 112-119
    configuring, 106-111
    exiting, 122
    restoring files, 120-121
Microsoft Publisher desktop publishing
        program, 210
modifier keys, 16-17
monitors, 12-13, 216
    starting, 32-33
    turning off, 36
mouse, 13, 217
Move command (DOS Shell File
        menu), 184-185
Move File (F7) shortcut key, 185
movement keys, 16-17
moving files in DOS Shell, 184-185
MSAV command, 123-125
MSBACKUP command, 104-111

N

naming files, 20-21, 94-95
    see also renaming files
Non-System disk or disk error
        error message, 33, 199
Not Ready reading drive A.
        Abort, Retry, Fail? error
        message, 76-77

P

PageMaker desktop publishing
        program, 210
Paradox database program, 206
Paradox for Windows database
        program, 206
PATH command, 22, 142-143
paths, 19, 142-143, 217
pausing file listing, 64-65
PC Paintbrush (draw) graphics
        program, 208
PC Week, 214
PC World, 214
Peachtree financial program, 212

Personal R:BASE database program,
206
PFS: First Publisher desktop
publishing program, 210
PFS: WindowWorks integrated
program, 211
PFS:First Choice integrated program,
211
PgDn/PgUp keys, 16
PowerPoint (charts) graphics program,
208
Press any key to continue error
message, 64
Print Screen key, 16
printers, 13
Professional Write word processing
program, 202
program list, 153
programs, 217
 communications, 210-211
 database, 206
 desktop publishing, 209-210
 DOS Shell, 152-153
 education, 213
 exiting, 36
 financial, 212
 games, 213
 graphics, 207-208
 integrated, 211
 MEMMAKER, 146-147
 MSAV, 123-125
 spreadsheets, 203-204
 VSAFE, 126-127
 word processing, 201-202
PROMPT command, 37-39, 198

Q

Q&A database program, 206
QuarkXpress desktop publishing
program, 210
Quattro Pro for Windows spreadsheet
program, 204
Quattro Pro spreadsheet program, 204
Quicken financial program, 212
Quicken for Windows financial
program, 212

R

RAM (random-access memory), 144,
217
RD command, 62-63, 198
removing, see deleting
RENAME command, 94-95, 198
Rename command (DOS Shell File
menu), 182-183
renaming files, 94-95, 182-183
Reset buttons, 34-35
RESTORE command, 198
restoring files, 120-122, 217
ROM (read-only memory), 144
root directories, 19, 54-55
 changing to, 58-59
 files, 48-49

S

scanning for viruses, 123-127
screens, clearing, 50-51
Scroll Lock key, 16
Search command (DOS Shell File
menu), 190-191
searching, see finding
Select All command (DOS Shell File
menu), 178-179
shells, see DOS Shell
Shift key, 16-17
shortcut keys
 Collapse Directory (-, minus), 165
 Expand Directory (*, asterisk), 163
 Expand Directory (+, plus), 163
 File Copy (F8), 181
 File Delete (Del), 187
 File Exit (Alt-F4), 157
 Move File (F7), 185
 View File Contents, 189
software, care and maintenance, 25
 see also programs
sorting files, 172-173
source disks, 80-81
spreadsheet programs, 203-204
starting
 DOS, 32-33
 DOS Shell, 152-153

subdirectories, 60-61
switches, /W, DIR command, 52-53
syntax, 25, 217
system unit, 12-13

T

target disks, 80-81
text-editing keys, 16-17
TIME command, 140-141, 198
times/dates, 32
    setting, 138-141
Too many parameters error message,
    67-68
TREE command, 60-61
trees, *see* directory trees
TSRs (terminate-and-stay-resident
    programs), VSAFE, 126-127
TurboTax financial program, 212
TYPE command, 84-85, 198

U–V

UNDELETE command, 100-101
undeleting files, 100-101
upper memory, 144

Ventura Publisher desktop publishing
    program, 210
VER command, 134-135
VERF command, 198
versions, DOS, 24, 134-135
View File Contents command (DOS
    Shell File menu), 188-189
View File Contents shortcut key, 189
viewing files in DOS Shell, 188-189
viruses, 217
    scanning, 123-127
VOL command, 130-131
volume labels, 75, 130-131
    changing, 132-133
VSAFE command, 126-127

W–Z

/W switch, DIR commands, 52-53
warm boots, 34-35
wide listing, files, 52-53
wild cards, 20-21, 66-67, 191, 217
    files, 171
Windows (Microsoft), 201
Windows Paintbrush graphics
    program, 208
Word for Windows (Microsoft), 202
word processing programs, 201-202
WordStar word processing program,
    202
WordPerfect for Windows word
    processing program, 202
WordPerfect Presentation graphics
    program, 208
WordPerfect word processing program,
    202
WordPerfect Works integrated
    program, 211